Investing in Change

Investing in Change

The reform of Europe's financial markets

EDITED BY ANDREW GOWERS

FOREWORD BY GAËL DE BOISSARD

HANS-PAUL BÜRKNER, HUGO DIXON,
TOM GOSLING, SIMON LEWIS, ALAN MORRISON,
AVINASH PERSAUD, MARTIN SORRELL,
PAUL TUCKER, SHRITI VADERA,
WILLIAM WILHELM, EDDY WYMEERSCH,
RUPERT YOUNGER

First published in Great Britain in 2012 by
The Association for Financial Markets in Europe (AFME)
St Michael's House
1 George Yard
London EC3V 9DH
in association with Profile Books Ltd

A CIP catalogue record for this book is available from the British Library.

ISBN 978 1 78125 013 6

Text design by Geoff Green
Typeset in Swift by MacGuru Ltd
info@macguru.org.uk

Printed and bound by CPI Group (UK)
Ltd, Croydon, CR0 4YY

Contents

The authors

Gaël de Boissard is chairman of the Association for Financial
Markets in Europe and a managing director at Credit Suisse in
the investment banking division, based in London. He is
co-head of global securities, a member of the investment bank
management committee and chair of the fixed income operating committee. Before that he held a variety of senior roles
within fixed income including head of global rates and foreign
exchange, and head of global securities for Europe, the Middle
East and Africa. He joined Credit Suisse First Boston in 2001
from J.P. Morgan, where he ran the European fixed income
business and was a member of the European Management
Committee. He joined J.P. Morgan's Paris office in 1990 and
held a number of trading positions in bonds, swaps, exotics
and proprietary trading.

Hans-Paul Bürkner has been president and chief executive officer
of the Boston Consulting Group (BCG) since 2003. He joined the
firm in 1981 and was a member of the teams that opened the
group's Düsseldorf (1982) and Frankfurt (1991) offices. Before
becoming BCG's first European chief executive officer, he was
head of the global financial institutions practice. During his
30 years at BCG, his clients have included many of the world's

leading financial institutions. He has worked with them to rede-
fine the competitive landscapes in their segments, helped them
to innovate their business models in their various business
activities, and spearheaded major global expansion initiatives.

Hugo Dixon is the founder, editor-in-chief and chairman at
Reuters Breakingviews, a leading international source of online
financial commentary. Before founding Breakingviews, he
spent 13 years at the *Financial Times*, the last five as head of Lex.
He began his journalistic career at *The Economist*.

Tom Gosling is a partner at PricewaterhouseCoopers and leader
of the firm's UK reward practice, advising companies and
remuneration committees on executive compensation. He has
worked extensively with banks and regulators on the remuneration response to the financial crisis. Prior to joining PwC
he was a research fellow in the Department of Applied Mathematics and Theoretical Physics at Cambridge University from
1994 to 1996.

Andrew Gowers, commissioning editor, is Strategic Communications Consultant to AFME and a former Editor of the *Financial
Times*.

Simon Lewis was appointed chief executive of AFME in October
2010. Previously he was director of communications and the
prime minister's official spokesman at 10 Downing Street. He
has held a number of senior corporate roles, including director
of corporate affairs at Vodafone, Centrica and NatWest. He was
appointed as the first communications secretary to the Queen
in 1998. He is a visiting fellow at Oxford University and at
Cardiff School of Journalism. He is also chairman of the Ful-
bright Commission and a member of the advisory board of the
National Portrait Gallery.

The authors

Alan Morrison is a fellow of Merton College Oxford and lectures in economics and management at Oxford University's Saïd Business School. His research interests lie mostly in the application of ideas from information economics to finance theory and to the economics of organisations. His research papers have covered subjects such as the interplay between moral hazard, adverse selection and optimal capital regulation for banks; risk-shifting effects in the presence of deposit insurance; credit derivatives; bank bail-out policy; financial panics and book-buildings in initial public offerings.

Avinash D. Persaud is chairman of Elara Capital, PBL and Intelligence Capital, and a board director of RBC Latin America & the Caribbean. Formerly, he was chairman of the Warwick Commission and the regulatory subcommittee of the UN High Level Task Force on Financial Reform; co-chair of the OECD's EmNet (Emerging Markets Network); and a member of the UK Treasury's Audit Committee, the intergovernmental task force on financial taxes and the Pew Task Force to the US Senate Banking Committee. He was also president of the British Association for the Advancement of Science (Section F) and a governor of the London School of Economics. He is Emeritus Professor at Gresham College, a fellow of London Business School and visiting fellow, CFAP, Judge Institute, Cambridge University. He was ranked the world's number two public intellectual on the financial crisis by an expert panel for *Prospect Magazine*.

Sir Martin Sorrell is founder and CEO of WPP. Under his leadership, the company has grown — by acquisition and organically — to become the world's largest communications services group, with over 153,000 people (including associates) working across some 150 companies in 107 countries.WPP companies, which include some of the most eminent agencies in the business, provide clients with advertising; media investment

ix

management; information; insight and consultancy; public relations and public affairs; branding and identity; healthcare communications; direct, digital, promotion and relationship marketing and specialist communications. Leading operating companies include JWT, Ogilvy, Y&R, Grey, GroupM, Millward Brown, TNS, Burson-Marsteller, Hill & Knowlton, Landor, Wunderman, CommonHealth, Blue State Digital and 24/7 Real Media.

Paul Tucker is deputy governor, financial stability, at the Bank of England, a post he has held since March 2009. He is a member of the Monetary Policy Committee, the Financial Policy Committee and the bank's Court of Directors. He also serves on the G20 Financial Stability Board's steering committee. From June 2002 to March 2009, he was executive director for markets. From January 1999, he was deputy director, financial stability, and was closely involved with the bank's Financial Stability Review. From May 1997 to June 2002, he was also on the secretariat of the Monetary Policy Committee, preparing the published minutes. He was head of the monetary assessment and strategy division, 1997 – 98, and principal private secretary to governor Robin Leigh-Pemberton for three and a half years until 1993, when he moved to the domestic market operations area. Before that he worked as a banking supervisor, a corporate financier at a merchant bank and on projects to reform the Hong Kong securities markets and regulatory system following the 1987 crash.

Baroness Shriti Vadera advises companies, funds and governments on strategy, finance and restructuring. During 2010 she advised the South Korean presidency of the G20 on formulating and negotiating policy outcomes for the G20 Seoul summit and the government of Dubai on the restructuring of Dubai World's debt. She currently advises Temasek Holdings, Singapore, and

Allied Irish Banks, and is a non-executive director of BHP Billiton and AstraZeneca. From June 2007 to September 2009 she was a minister in the UK government's Cabinet Office and Departments for Business and International Development. She worked on the government's response to the financial crisis, was a key architect of the UK bank recapitalisation plan, and devised and helped negotiate the outcomes of the April 2009 G20 London summit, which the IMF described as 'breaking the fall in the global economy'. She was on HM Treasury's Council of Economic Advisers from 1999 to 2007, working on business and international economic and finance issues. Before that she was an investment banker for 14 years with SG Warburg/UBS focusing on emerging markets.

William J. Wilhelm Jr is William G. Shenkir Eminent Scholar at the University of Virginia's McIntire School of Commerce. He is an investment banking specialist whose teaching interests include corporate finance and financial engineering. His research focuses on the investment banking industry, and his work has been published in many journals, including *The American Economic Review*, *Journal of Financial Economics*, *Journal of Money, Credit, and Banking* and *Oxford Review of Economic Policy*. In his book *Information Markets* (Harvard Business School Press, 2001), he explains how advances in IT are transforming financial markets. His latest book, *Investment Banking: Institutions, Politics, and Law* (Oxford University Press, 2007), is an economic history of the investment banking industry. Before joining McIntire, he held the American Standard Companies Chair in Management Studies at Saïd Business School, University of Oxford; he has also has held visiting appointments at the Institut d'Economie Industrielle (IDEI) in Toulouse, France, and at the Federal Home Loan Mortgage Corporation. He has worked as a consultant for the Resolution Trust Corporation, Dresdner Securities, London Economics and Oxford Economic Research Associates.

Eddy Wymeersch is chairman of the Public Interest Oversight Board, overseeing standard-setting in the field of auditing. He is a member of the board of FINMA in Berne and of the Qatar Financial Regulatory Authority. He has been chairman of the Committee of European Securities Regulators (CESR; February 2007–July 2010) and of the European Regional Committee of IOSCO, in that capacity also taking part in the executive and the technical committee (2006–10). He was chief executive (2001–07) and chairman of the supervisory board (2007–10) of the Belgian Commission Bancaire, Financière et des Assurances (CBFA). Before joining the CBFA, he held public posts in Belgium, including 'regent' of the National Bank of Belgium and member of the legislative branch of the Council of State. He has served on the boards of several Belgian companies and was chairman of Brussels airport. He has been an academic at Ghent Law School, where he founded the Financial Law Institute, and has served on several committees advising the Belgian government. He has acted as an adviser to the European Commission and several European financial institutions and stock exchanges, and a consultant to the World Bank and IFC. He has published extensively on company law, corporate governance and financial regulation and is a member of the European Corporate Governance Forum.

Rupert Younger is the founder director of the Oxford University Centre for Corporate Reputation based at Oxford University's Saïd Business School. Established in 2008, the centre undertakes research and teaching on how corporations and institutions create, sustain, destroy and rebuild reputation. He is also a co-founder of the Finsbury Group, a financial communications group with offices in London, New York and Brussels, and remains a consulting partner. He has 20 years' experience in financial communications, working with big UK and international companies on their financial communications, investor relations and reputation engagement programmes. He is a specialist in international IPOs and mergers and acquisitions, having led many of Finsbury's major transactions.

Figures

Foreword

GAËL DE BOISSARD

CHAIRMAN, ASSOCIATION FOR FINANCIAL MARKETS IN EUROPE

These are tumultuous times for Europe's banking industry and financial markets. The financial crisis that erupted in 2008 has rarely been out of the headlines since. What started as a problem in US housing finance became a global banking crash which caused grave economic damage and a massive call on the public purse on both sides of the Atlantic. By 2011, the pressure on public purses was nowhere more obvious than in Europe, with the stability of the global financial system and the future of the European single currency at stake.

Yet this has not been a period solely of upheaval and crisis management. It has also been a time of reform. It has featured rigorous self-examination by the banks themselves; tough scrutiny by government authorities and politicians and interest groups of many stripes; and above all a widespread determination to ensure that a crisis of these dimensions should never be allowed to recur. Regulators, governments, bank boards, shareholders and clients have been working on measures to create a safer financial system. The common goal is banks that are better managed, governed and regulated — and capable of winning back public confidence as a vital engine of growth in the European economy.

This may seem a daunting challenge at a time of public

anger at what has gone wrong in the system — and at the role of the banks in particular. But it is a cause central to the existence of the Association for Financial Markets in Europe (AFME), as the representative body for Europe's wholesale financial markets and those who trade in and service them. It is also why we have commissioned this book of essays on European financial reform and the outlook for the region's banking industry.

Three years after the crisis began, with a significant regulatory overhaul on the books and in the pipeline, we wanted to stand back and take stock of where the industry has come from and where it is going. And we decided not to make the assessment ourselves or through the eyes of our member firms, but to ask respected independent authorities to write essays on different aspects of the subject as they see it.

What has changed in management and oversight of wholesale financial services — from regulation through risk management to remuneration? What still needs to change? What have we learned from the crisis and from the efforts to reshape the sector in its wake? What issues need to be addressed to revitalise Europe's capital markets? What are the challenges that lie ahead for the regulators and the regulated?

Not surprisingly, the picture that emerges in this book is of a deeply challenging and uncertain environment. But two generally positive developments can be discerned.

First, the past three years have seen tremendous change in the way financial firms are regulated. The amounts of capital and liquidity that banks are being obliged to hold have risen dramatically. Leverage, an indicator of balance-sheet risk, has been reduced. Market infrastructures have been substantially strengthened, with the centralised clearing of derivatives perhaps the most obvious example. Overall, regulatory frameworks have been enhanced at firm and industry level and governments and regulators are increasingly emphasising the importance of 'macroprudential' supervision to respond to real-economy risks arising from the financial sector.

Second, firms themselves have undertaken significant internal reforms and balance-sheet restructuring. Optimistic risk assessment and risk management were at the root of the 2008 financial crisis. Corporate governance and internal procedures have been bolstered in response. Risk management is no longer regarded as a subset of the compliance function: in most firms it is now at the heart of the decision-making process within the firm and on corporate boards. These systems are not yet fail-safe, but they are much stronger and are continuing to improve. Lastly, significant changes have already been introduced in remuneration policies and practices, even though we suspect there is more to do.

Making such progress has required a lot of hard work on the part of all involved, and I believe AFME, with its deep industry expertise and close connectivity with its member firms, has played a constructive part in implementing these improvements. Nevertheless, we have to admit that the changes in themselves do not get us all the way there. Neither the industry nor its regulators are yet in a position to declare 'mission accomplished'.

Moreover, intense public controversy continues to rage about everything from the role of bankers in the crisis, through the adequacy of remedies that have been offered to date, to the nature of the relationships between banks and society and between financial markets and the real economy. These debates will remain at the centre of our political and economic lives in Europe for some time to come.

This is why I believe that the changes we have seen are just the beginning of an even more arduous process that will fundamentally reshape our financial markets and leave a profound mark on all who work in them. I would like to explain why I believe that to be so and pose some questions to the industry, to those who oversee it and to all those who feel they have a stake in its future.

The three most important questions are these:

- What does society want from its wholesale banking industry?
- How does banking reshape itself to deliver what society wants?
- How do we articulate the relationship between banks and society — or between the markets and the economy — in a new and more sustainable way?

Finding candid and credible answers to all three is vital for the future of Europe's banking industry, which, after all, employs more than 3 million people and contributes 6.5 per cent to the region's GDP. But it matters even more than that. Because of banks' wider role in financing business and consumption and the way the health of banks is inextricably bound up with the health of the wider economy, answering these questions is equally central to the tasks of creating stability, resolving our problems with private and public debt, and generating growth and jobs.

Such has been the tumult in and around the industry in the past two years that establishing a measured and rational discussion of these issues has been exceptionally hard.

For one thing, the market pressures have been intense. Banks, facing a veritable tsunami of new regulations imposed by multifarious governments and agencies on both sides of the Atlantic, have struggled to keep up. Managers are overloaded, compliance costs are rising, and the overall coherence of the system can sometimes seem hard to discern. Meanwhile, investors have tended to price in regulatory impacts as if they were immediate, rather than discounting for any notional lead-times allowed for implementation. The new Basel III capital regime is the most obvious example. The lead-time built in, allowing participants until 2019 to adapt, has all but disappeared: banks have to act as if it is now fully in force.

Perhaps it is not surprising that senior bank executives sometimes sound as if they are resisting change in principle. My observation is that most of them are not, but some are wilting under the strain of so much rapid change. And as the dust begins to settle, it is entirely legitimate for the industry to ask searching questions about the overall coherence of a system patched together from the competing and sometimes contra-dictory demands of many different governments and legisla-tors. We are still some way from having any kind of sense of their cumulative impact, and this is in itself a concern.

Then there is the critical political climate. I am not com-plaining about it; it is a fact. But it can distort discussions about such important matters as regulation or taxation of banks. Instead of considering how to create the optimal framework that will encourage banks to fulfil their economic function, decision-makers find it tempting to court easy popularity by appearing to punish the sector or to pile punitive taxation on top of regulation. The European Union's mooted financial transactions tax is a classic example. All recent studies on the subject, including the European Commission's own impact study, demonstrate that such a tax would create serious eco-nomic damage for questionable benefit. Yet European govern-ments press ahead.

In my personal view, the sound and fury around these issues of regulatory practice and political expediency obscure two much broader and more challenging sets of arguments, espe-cially for those who manage, oversee and indeed invest in banks. The first has to do with the culture of banking itself — the way banks are run, the way bankers behave, and what needs to be done to effect deep and lasting change in both. The second concerns the desirable shape, scale, scope and revenue-generating capacity of the industry.

Let me take each in turn. There is no doubt that the culture of banks has changed profoundly in the past 20 years. When I joined the Paris office of a large investment bank in 1990, the compliance or risk departments were less elaborate, let's say, given the smaller and less complex institutions of the time. The operating assumptions had to do with individual and collective responsibility. In today's giant financial conglomerates, part of that sense of responsibility has been lost or taken away — not least by ever-increasing regulation and the ever-present slogan 'too big to fail'.

The question is: even if large publicly quoted banking groups cannot possibly turn the clock back and reinvent themselves as private partnerships, how can they recapture some of that old spirit of partnership and responsibility in the way they run their affairs? Doing so would have far-reaching effects on the business. It would imply, for example, a bias against complex financial products that only a small number of aficionados can fully understand. It would suggest that institutions would not create financial instruments that they would not be willing to hold on their books. It would drive remuneration and other management policies towards a system that gives employees a deep sense of individual and collective commitment in the way they do their jobs — a real sense that they have 'skin in the game'. The alternative is banking as a regulated utility of sorts.

The point I am making is about management and govern-ance, but it has important implications for the political debate that portrays banks as public enemy number one. If banks are perceived to be embracing profound change of the kind I have outlined, then the industry's reputation will steadily improve. It will become possible to think in terms of what I would call a new settlement between the industry and society, in which bankers come to be seen again as responsible citizens playing a crucial economic role without the need for controversial gov-ernment support.

I believe that is the direction we will take — though of course it will take time for the trend to become visible, and longer still for public perceptions to undergo fundamental change for the better. This is the work of years, not weeks or months. It is, incidentally, a journey that needs to be taken not only by bankers but also by all the other players who got it wrong during the boom years — governments, regulators, supranational institutions, shareholders. Everyone has lessons to learn from a crisis this profound.

As to the scale and scope of banking institutions, we are, I suspect, in the early stages of a similarly seismic change. The portents of this are all around us. Governments everywhere are looking for ways to limit taxpayers' potential risk exposure — either by limiting the size of banking institutions for which they are responsible, or by ring-fencing different segments of the institutions' activities, or by otherwise constraining those of their activities perceived as being especially risky.

Politicians, regulators and banks in the UK, France, Germany and other European countries are engaged in difficult debates about risk, reward and the allocation of resources — not least in lending to the real economy. Banks and their shareholders are beginning in similarly awkward ways to tussle over the uses and cost of capital and the desirable returns on its deployment. Others question the very right of global universal banks to exist, and call for a return to a simpler though perhaps less risky world of specialism and national or regional focus.

No one can know for sure what the outcome of these processes will be. But together they are generating a series of compelling and utterly necessary debates about the role of banks in a modern economy.

One example is the discussion that took place in the UK during the last few weeks of 2011 concerning banks' risk appetite, remuneration and shareholder returns. Critics of the banks maintained that if only banks would put their remuneration and risk-taking houses in order, they could raise capital from investors and boost lending to the economy. Representatives of the banks, including AFME, responded by pointing out that the problem with this argument is the low returns currently on offer to investors, which make expanding the loan book an unattractive proposition for banks and pumping in further equity a deeply unappealing prospect for investors.

The debate is complex, and is certainly not all one way. But I believe that calm and dispassionate analysis of the facts is an essential precursor to the banking industry's return to health. I hope that this will eventually lead to a better and safer world, in which systemic leverage is reduced, regulation is optimised, and banks can resume their traditional role as enablers of payment flows and economic growth without recourse to the support of governments and taxpayers. Let's make this the new normal, in welcome contrast to the abnormal circumstances of recent years.

This book is intended as an important contribution to the debate and analysis. In concluding, it remains for me to thank the contributors who worked hard, often under extreme deadline pressures, to deliver such a cogent and well-written set of essays; the editors responsible for commissioning the chapters and readying them for publication; and the many other people who have had a hand in bringing this project to fruition. I look forward to continuing these discussions and thus helping to create a stronger and more resilient financial system with a robust, proportionate and sustainable regulatory regime.

Gaël de Boissard
January 2012

Introduction

It is a truism that liquid capital markets and a well-functioning banking system are the beating heart of any successful modern economy. And whatever else may be said about the economic predicament in which we find ourselves in Europe, no one can seriously pretend that the capital markets or the banking system have been functioning as they should in the past several years.

This book is an exploration of what has gone wrong and of the efforts that are under way to put it right, published under the auspices of the organisation representing the leading European and global banks active in the wholesale markets, the Association for Financial Markets in Europe (AFME).

I hope readers will quickly realise it is not propaganda. It is a serious collection of essays about reform and regulation of banks and markets, written by acknowledged and independent authorities: regulators, consultants, academics and others. We want it to be read by practitioners, politicians, journalists, activists and anyone else with an interest in the return to health of this crucial industry.

Why has AFME decided to publish such a volume? Because we think the debates currently under way about the future of financial markets in Europe are of significant public interest and that the experts whose work is on display in these pages have an important contribution to make.

The reason for AFME's existence is to provide a practical, constructive market view to policymakers and the public on the significant, and necessary, reforms taking place in the financial system. We can offer this insight because we directly represent market participants and can deploy the expertise of our members and partners to address market challenges. And we do so in a constant and close partnership with regulators, governments and others whose job it is to oversee the markets and our member firms.

The book marks an extension of that mission. It is designed both to illustrate the fundamental changes that are under way in banking and the markets and to indicate where further change may still be needed. It aims to engage with the banking industry's critics as well as to enlighten its friends. Above all, we want to demonstrate that as a sector we embrace change – indeed, as the title suggests, are investing in it – and are aware that it is a dynamic process with a lot of road still to travel.

The opinions and arguments expressed in the rest of this book are attributable to the authors alone. By definition, AFME will not agree with everything they say, but it respects all the points of view assembled here and plans to work with the authorities and other stakeholders to ensure continuing progress towards a safe and viable financial sector at the heart of a thriving European and global economy.

To produce a rounded picture, we have deliberately sought a broad range of perspectives. We start with one of the UK's and Europe's most important financial regulators, Paul Tucker, deputy governor, financial stability, at the Bank of England and a key member of the Financial Stability Board that was set up by the Group of 20 leaders in 2008 to reform regulation in the wake of the crisis. He offers an incisive overview of financial regulation in the past three decades before explaining the priorities on the global reform agenda and how they fit together.

Market economies, he argues, cannot succeed without a safe and sound banking sector and an effective and efficient financial system. In the recent past, regulation has failed to keep up with the progressive fusion of banking, capital markets and insurance. Now, he concludes, credible reform is crucial to restoring confidence and creating sustainable economic growth.

Baroness Shriti Vadera is another important witness to recent policymaking. As a minister in the last Labour government under Gordon Brown, she was a key member of the prime minister's crisis management team as the financial storm broke, and was centrally involved as the G20 launched its drive to improve regulation of the financial sector and to ensure, in the words of the summit declaration, 'that a global crisis, such as this one, does not happen again'. Her contribution holds the G20 to account against this demanding benchmark and analyses the imperfect track record of international co-operation to date.

One of the most important areas for change in the management and regulation of banks emerging from the crisis concerns oversight of risk. Flaws in risk management were at the centre of what happened and in chapter 3, Eddy Wymeersch takes a look at Europe's efforts to address these flaws. An experienced regulator, he was chairman of the Committee of European Securities Regulators from 2007 to 2010, and so helped shape the European response as the crisis unfolded. He gives a detailed and expert view of the emerging EU legislative landscape and the sweeping changes in banks' risk management now taking shape as a result.

Another controversial topic for bank executives and those who oversee them has been remuneration. Many observers have argued that distorted short-term incentives were in part responsible for the financial excesses that prompted the crisis, and this has been a key focus for regulators. As a result, a sweeping reform of remuneration practices is under way, including improved governance, better alignment between remuneration and risk management, and a restructuring of pay packages. Tom Gosling, a partner at Pricewaterhouse-Coopers and leader of the firm's UK reward practice, assesses the progress in chapter 4. 'Compensation did not create the credit crunch,' he concludes, 'but it did add fuel to the fire.' We can therefore expect regulators to maintain an interest in the subject for the foreseeable future.

The effects of the market turmoil have, of course, reached well beyond the financial sector itself, and no European company has been left untouched. Many corporate executives have been watching events with great concern, wondering whether policymakers can really make the financial system safer and what impact they will have on the real economy as they try. For a corporate perspective, we asked Sir Martin Sorrell, chief executive of global communications services group WPP, to give his assessment of reform efforts. It is a sombre one: he worries that governments and bank executives alike have not learned the right lessons from the crisis, and he laments the lack of political leadership in managing it so far.

Chapter 6 looks beyond the immediate crisis and regulatory response to the broader changes likely to affect Europe's financial sector in the coming years courtesy of Hans-Paul Bürkner, president and CEO of the Boston Consulting Group. He has a wealth of experience of the financial services sector and sees a wide range of daunting challenges facing it, from slow economic growth and intense competition at home through the rise of new economic powers to wrenching technological upheaval. He describes a 'new normal financial environment' in which capital is more expensive, many traditionally profitable activities become uneconomic, and balance-sheet management and risk control are all-important differentiators. 'The only certainty seems to be a volatile and intense competitive climate,' he writes.

One of the concerns frequently expressed by company executives — and not only those in the financial services sector — is the danger of 'regulatory overshoot': the idea that the crisis will prompt the pendulum to swing from the so-called 'light-touch' regulation of the pre-crisis years to a much more onerous system that will throttle beneficial economic activity and financial innovation. This is the focus of chapter 7, contributed by Avinash Persaud, chairman of financial firms Intelligence Capital and Elara Capital, former head of research at State Street Bank and a regular adviser to governments on financial issues. He seeks to expose some of the popular myths about the causes of the crisis, and warns against heavy-handed interventions in markets that some authorities appear tempted to consider — measures such as bans on short-selling or restrictions on derivatives trading.

Another big challenge facing bank executives is rebuilding the reputation of their firms. But there is an important debate to be had about precisely what this means. In chapter 8, three academic authors, Alan Morrison, William Wilhelm and Rupert Younger, argue that the subject is by no means as clear-cut as it may seem. Changes in market practices, they argue, reflect deep and irreversible technological changes that have altered the role and relevance of reputation in banking and have also created new conflicts of interest that are hard to resolve, not only for bankers but also for regulators.

Ultimately, the issue of responsibility for the crisis — of who is to blame and in what measure — remains perhaps the hottest subject in a debate that shows no sign of abating. AFME is acutely aware of the criticisms that continue to be levelled at the banking sector. I do not propose to wade into the controversy in this introduction, but as a sign that we acknowledge the issues we commissioned Hugo Dixon, a leading financial journalist and editor-in-chief of the Breakingviews online commentary service, to give his own perspective. His light-hearted response is '*Nostra culpa*', an imaginary letter of apology to the G20 from a fictitious bank executive by the name of Humboldt Pye.

I would like to add my sincere thanks to the AFME board and its chairman Gaël de Boissard, who gave this project their strong support from the outset; to Andrew Gowers, who as commissioning editor made it happen; and to all the contributors and others who gave valuable time and insights. I hope that readers will find the book useful, insightful, informative — and even in parts provocative. We wanted to give regulators, politicians, finance professionals, those contemplating a financial career and interested members of the public a sense of the challenges facing the financial sector as a result of the crisis and how it is responding.

We would like to use the publication to initiate a broad debate on these issues and on how a revived banking sector can contribute to a healthy European economy. I would welcome comments from any interested party. Please email your views to publications@afme.eu.

Simon Lewis
January 2012

1

Banking in a market economy – the international agenda

PAUL TUCKER

The central challenge of the programme for reforming the global financial system is to return banking to its rightful place in a market economy. Mainstream policymakers and bankers of all persuasions are surely united in this: that banking should not depend on a safety net from taxpayers. Those who most espouse the disciplines of capitalism – bankers and financiers – should live by them.

Banks of all shapes and sizes are levered, run maturity mismatches, lend to risky borrowers and are highly interconnected. The reform programme will moderate but not abolish this. So, like any business, banks can fail. But, unlike many businesses, they can fall like dominos, with big economic and social costs. All this – neglected for so long – is now again driving policy, thank goodness.

The solutions have to be international, global. We live in a world where capital can flow freely across borders. This is good for economic prosperity; and it is good for freedom. But, together with a pronounced drift in Western economies towards relying on rules, it has made highly complex forms of regulatory arbitrage endemic — hence the desire among policymakers for a level playing field of strong minimum standards. For this reason alone, whichever capital city one sits in, the international reform programme is central. This piece gives my perspective on this work, being taken forward under the leadership of the G20-sponsored Financial Stability Board (FSB).

A generation or so ago, we could have relied upon separate regimes for banking and for securities markets. In that far-off world, banks extended and held illiquid loans, overseen by banking supervisors. And, in a largely separate universe, securities regulators policed the integrity of individual transactions and offerings on public exchanges served by specialist intermediaries. The growth of private markets, over-the-counter derivatives, securitisation and of banks as intermediaries in capital markets has changed all that, as the 2007 – 09 crisis cruelly exposed. The revolution, whether we like it or not, has been the fusion of banking and capital markets. Even the most limited forms of commercial banking involve hedging of customer business in interest-rate and foreign-exchange markets. Wholesale loans to medium-sized and large companies — loans that are syndicated and traded — lie in the intersection of commercial and investment banking. The solutions to the problems of global finance have to cover securities markets as well as banking.

In consequence, on top of the crucial and extensive repairs to existing regulatory regimes, the international reform programme has had to embrace three new elements:

- Solve too big to fail: resolution
- Simplify capital-market networks: central counterparties, and more
- Take a system-wide view: macroprudential

Fault lines in the old international regulatory regime for banks

Before reviewing the new world, it is worth pausing to recognise the fault lines in the regulatory regime for banks prevailing in the crucial decade or so during which the present crisis was brewed.

Five are worth dwelling on. Four affect the regime for capital. In terms of true ability to absorb losses, capital is set to increase by perhaps as much as an order of magnitude relative to risk-weighted assets — which, incidentally, will in the first instance reduce headline returns on equity and, prospectively, the split of profits between managers and shareholders. The fifth fault line concerns liquidity (or, rather, the lack of it).

Leverage ratios versus risk-asset ratios

Currently, it is a commonplace that risk-based capital ratios are deeply flawed — because the measurement of risk is inevitably flawed and, worse, exposed to abuses by bankers and their advisers. This is true. Leverage ratios offer a simple constraint on balance-sheet expansion.

Twenty-five years ago, it was a commonplace that leverage ratios were deeply flawed — because they gave bankers a strong incentive to book assets that were both more risky than the regulators had had in mind when they calibrated their leverage rule and riskier than the regulators and creditors could easily spot. This was, and is, true. It was why Paul Volcker, chairman of the Federal Reserve Board, suggested to Robin Leigh-Pemberton, governor of the Bank of England, in the mid-1980s that there should be joint work on a full-blown system of risk-based capital requirements. That led to the first Basel Capital Accord.

Looking back on the past 25 – 30 years, I conclude that both these commonplace judgements are true. But we do not need to choose. We need both a risk-based capital requirement and, as a backstop, a leverage limit. That is precisely what Basel III incorporates.

What is capital? Basel I's mistake

The state regulates and supervises banks because the social costs of bank failure exceed the private costs to equity holders, creditors and managers — so-called 'negative externalities'. And no one should doubt this after the current crisis. In consequence, the state steps in to establish, among other things, minimum capital requirements.

This regime barely functions if the instruments that count, for regulatory purposes, as capital do not, in fact, absorb losses in a going concern and so cannot keep a loss-making bank out of liquidation. Yet, tragically, that is exactly where we found ourselves. The first Basel Capital Accord opened a door to 'hybrid' instruments. Most of them — and, as the years passed, supervisors around the world permitted more and more of them — offered leverage to equity holders (and to managers holding equity options) but provided no protection to ordinary creditors outside insolvent liquidation.

Thus one crucial repair to the Basel Capital Accord is that, basically, only common equity will be counted as 'core' capital by bank supervisors in future.

The measurement of risk in risk-based capital requirements

Over the past 15 years or so, officials and bankers — and, in a related sphere, insurers — have become overexcited about precise measurements of risk. Advances in finance theory and computing power led too many to believe that the risks to which banks are exposed could be measured 'scientifically'. What this lacked was any of the disciplined scepticism that is, surely, the animating spirit of science. It was as if a bunch of finance economists had inhaled the dogmatic rather than the enquiring spirit of the Enlightenment and breathed it into a

18

load of popular science. That cultural risk persists.

The reliance on internal models overlooked a host of things:

- the short runs of data from which the models were calibrated;
- the presence of strategic interaction in capital markets, which can cause forced selling by herds;
- the related possibility that liquidity in a market can dry up, causing liquidity premiums to soar, and thus asset prices and firms' (mark-to-market) net worth to collapse;
- the principal – agent problems between bank boards, senior executives and the risk modellers themselves, especially if the modellers are close to desk-heads in the firms.

Quite a lot has been done already or is under way to remedy these problems. Basel 2.5 provides a partial correction of some technical mistakes. A more fundamental review of capital requirements for the trading book is under way, including catering for the risk of jumps in liquidity premiums. And the Basel Committee on Banking Supervision (BCBS) is planning an exercise to compare the integrity of risk models across banks and jurisdictions – a legitimate question posed by some bankers. Interestingly, through the Dodd-Frank Act, the US has placed a Basel I-based minimum on the risk weights for different types of exposure.

But beyond all these measures is something else. However well-grounded any calibration of risk, circumstances will eventually arise where it is wrong, and clearly wrong. It is a great mistake for regulators to impale the stability of the system on a set of ostensibly timeless, static capital requirements. Risks and perceptions of risk inevitably change over time, sometimes beyond any range previously envisaged. This is one of the two underlying insights that drive the macroprudential agenda, as I discuss below.

Capital is there to be used: minima versus buffers

Both the first and second Basel Capital Accords were expressed as minima. In an environment that became progressively more reliant on rulebooks, this meant that there were express or implied sanctions for going below the minimum capital ratio. In other words, regulators were aiming to set capital at a higher level than the market would choose, but the capital they required could not be used.

In Basel III, the capital requirement is, for the first time, separated into a buffer and a base minimum. The minimum is designed to be broadly the level below which a normal bank could not operate; that is, the point at which 'resolution' beckons. The crucial new element is the usable buffer. The authorities will need to demonstrate that it is, truly, usable. I doubt that formulaic approaches will work.

This underlines the importance of reinjecting judgement into prudential supervision. Without elaborating on it here, this is absolutely the vision and plan for the UK's new Prudential Regulation Authority, which will be part of the Bank of England once the legislation passes through Parliament.[1]

Liquidity matters too

The Basel Committee was established following the collapse of Bankhaus Herstatt in the mid-1970s. The same crisis prompted the central bank governors' meeting in Basel to have an extended, intimate exchange on how their lender of last resort functions fit together in a world of cross-border, international banking.

This makes it all the more remarkable that in its first 35 years the supervisors' committee did not lay down more than high-level qualitative guidelines for banks' liquidity.[2]

The appalling result was that, by 2007, many banks were perilously reliant on short-term money-market funding. Few held a stock of truly liquid assets. And, perhaps worst of all, the 'treasury' portfolios of many medium-size banks, notably in the UK, comprised paper issued by other banks. At the level of the system as a whole, this was illusory liquidity. Such 'inside' instruments should not count towards banks' liquidity buffers.

What should count is a difficult question, and one that has been causing some angst recently given the realisation that even sovereign bonds can become impaired and illiquid. Unlike the role of equity in capital adequacy, there is no asset on earth that anyone can guarantee will be liquid in all seasons. Except one, that is. Provided central banks sustain low and stable inflation, and thus confidence in their currencies, central bank reserves are the ultimate liquid asset. Indeed, the whole point of a liquidity buffer is that banks should hold a stock of assets that can readily be converted via the market into central bank money – each economy's final settlement asset. Therefore if there is occasionally a shortage of other truly liquid assets, banks could simply hold more central bank reserves temporarily. The demand for central bank reserves reflects the desire of banks to hold central bank balances as a liquidity buffer; and central banks have to supply these reserves to ensure that overnight money-market rates are in line with their policy rates.

Too big to fail

However good the reforms described above are in the microregulatory regime for banks, they – and, indeed, any system of prophylactic regulation and supervision – will eventually be found wanting. Banks and dealers will fail.

The highest priority is to put in place a credible regime for managing the orderly failure of banks and other financial institutions, however large, complex or international. In other words, we absolutely must solve the too-big-to-fail problem.

Orderly failure of banks and dealers: resolution

Where losses exceed equity but outside capital cannot be raised, any kind of business must either go into liquidation or be reconstructed in some way. In the case of banking — and of other, highly levered dealers with illiquid assets — liquidation entails huge costs, a wasteful destruction of value, and disorder as financial contracts are closed out and essential services — payments, credit, risk transfer — are shut down. Regular liquidation will not do.

But reconstruction cannot involve taxpayer solvency support if banking is to remain a properly capitalist enterprise. This is why the FSB has focused on so-called resolution regimes. Stripping away all the detail, they are about spreading losses across creditors through a process that, so far as possible, preserves continuity of those essential services and functions. If one thing has to be achieved, this is it.

In November 2011, the G20 leaders endorsed a new International Standard for Resolution Regimes. As the then FSB chairman, Mario Draghi, has said, this is a breakthrough. The G20 countries have agreed to legislate to put a common resolution regime in place; to remove impediments to cross-border co-operation; and to embrace some incentives for home and host authorities to co-operate. 'Standard' is a term of art in the official world: it means that G20 countries have committed to implement the agreement, and that the IMF will report publicly on what countries have done. No one should doubt the commitment to make progress. In the EU, the European Commission's forthcoming draft directive — requiring member states to introduce highly developed resolution regimes — will, I believe, demonstrate the momentum that exists internationally.

Belt and braces (and some straps too)

But, of course, international policymakers would not sensibly rely on just one set of measures. And we have not done so. The reform agenda is, therefore, much richer.

When the FSB strategy was being developed, we talked openly about a belt-and-braces approach:

- introduce a capital surcharge, of up to 3.5 per cent of risk-weighted assets, to enhance the capital resources of those financial firms whose disorderly failure would carry the greatest economic and social costs and which are typically hardest to 'resolve' using existing technology – so-called systemically important financial institutions (SIFIs); and
- develop those enhanced resolution regimes in profound ways, so that we can resolve SIFIs in future.

We – the international policymakers – have been asked by the industry, repeatedly and not unreasonably, to introduce an explicit trade-off between the resolvability of a SIFI and the extent, if any, of the capital surcharge. At one level, we have declined to do so – we are not prepared to release SIFIs from a capital surcharge on the basis of an as yet untested resolution regime. Perhaps I should say that, as the chairman of the FSB's Resolution Steering Group, I was an active advocate of that position.

But at another level, we have implicitly accepted that resolvability should make a difference. Had we not believed that a robust resolution regime for global SIFIs could and would be developed and used, the pressures for a higher capital surcharge would have been greater.

Banks' capital structure: resolution redux

Imagine that a large, complex, global group has 20 lines of business, each the same size – that is to say, using the same amount of balance sheet and capital. Imagine it is 50 times levered. Now imagine that one of those lines of business is completely toxic, worthless. The firm is insolvent, bankrupt. Unless it can be resolved, it must cease trading and go into insolvent liquidation.

However, in this example only a single line of business is toxic; the other 19 are fine. In other words, the franchise has value. In the non-financial corporate sector, the remedy would be a negotiated reconstruction of the firm's capital structure, writing off the equity and partially converting debt claims into new equity. In banking, there is not time for a process involving negotiations between the parties under the jurisdiction of the courts. An administrative agency needs to make and execute some rapid judgements. This is precisely what so-called bail-in via resolution is about. Under the provisions of the FSB Resolution Standard, recapitalisation through reconstruction of liabilities can also prospectively cut through a number of the long-standing impediments to resolution stemming from conflicts between home and host country insolvency laws.

A misconception has, however, crept into some commentary about this: that 'bail-in' is the only mechanism through which unsecured, uninsured creditors will be exposed to loss. This, of course, is nonsense. Any resolution mechanism has that effect. The difference between different resolution tools lies in the process through which creditors discover their losses.

Taking the stylised example above, if it is unclear just how many of the distressed firm's business lines are badly infected, 'bail-in' may not be the best tool because the resolution authority would be uncertain beforehand which businesses to write off and thus about how far to write down debt contracts in order to recapitalise the firm. These are circumstances where the best course may be for the resolution authority to split the firm's essential services, such as deposit-taking and payments, from those that need to be carefully wound down.

The proposals of the UK's Independent Commission on Banking work with the grain of that. But no one underestimates the challenge in achieving a controlled wind-down of a trading book. It would be enormously aided by clearing up the organisational and financial structures of individual SIFIs – scaling back the number of legal entities and simplifying intra-group exposures and guarantees. Prudential supervisors are going to have to deliver on that important substantive challenge.

It would also be aided by simplifying the network of exposures among different firms in capital markets. And that is the second great venture of the international reform programme.

Simplifying capital market networks

Financial stability prevails where the financial system is sufficiently resilient that worries about bad states of the world do not undermine confidence in the ability of the system to deliver its core services to the rest of the economy.[3]

Those core services are the transfer of payments, the provision and intermediation of credit and equity, and risk transfer or insurance.

It is too easy to think about this purely in terms of individual firms. Firms are linked by markets and infrastructure – through a network of contracts covering derivatives; repos (repurchase agreements) and securities lending; correspondent banking, clearing and prime brokerage services; and so on. Furthermore, some markets are important in and of themselves because they bring together end-user savers and issuers of securities (bonds and equities). A financial-stability regime that focused solely on the safety and soundness of firms would be myopic.

This means enhancing the transparency of capital markets – around both primary and secondary markets. And it means direct action to simplify the network of financial exposures among banks and dealers and funds.

One relatively simple action, under discussion at the BCBS, would be to apply tighter controls to large exposures among SIFIs than to other unsecured interbank exposures. In principle, I would favour that. On a second front, central banks can, and should, play a more active role in monitoring and fostering robust practices and infrastructure in the short-term financing markets — repo, securities lending, commercial paper, and so on.

But, to date, the big project has been to move the main over-the-counter derivatives markets on to central infrastructure.

Central counterparties and, again, resolution
Central counterparties (CCPs) simplify the complex web of counterparty exposures through multilateral netting — precisely what the US authorities contemplated trying to achieve in an ad hoc way towards the end of the weekend over which Lehman Brothers was slipping away. But CCPs do more than facilitate multilateral netting. They substitute themselves as the counterparty to the trades they clear — hence a central counterparty.

That makes it more important than ever that the CCPs are themselves safe and sound. Three clearing houses have failed in recent decades. In 1974, the Caisse de Liquidation failed in Paris, due to default on margin calls when sugar-futures prices fell sharply. In 1983, it was the turn of the Kuala Lumpur Commodities Clearing House, when half a dozen large brokers defaulted following a crash in palm-oil futures. And, most dramatically, the Hong Kong Futures Exchange clearing house failed in the wake of the global stock-market crash in 1987. The effects were devastating. Both the futures exchange and the stock market had to close. Reopening the markets was no small feat.

As the post-1987 crash Hong Kong Securities Review Committee commented in the summer of 1988, nearly a quarter of a century ago:[4]

> *When everything else is stripped away, the most pressing issue is the management of risk. The focus of this is … increasingly, the central clearing houses – indeed [their] prudent operation is perhaps the single most important objective for the market authorities and regulators.*

As with banks, public policy for CCPs has to have two components. The first is minimum standards to ensure that CCPs are unlikely to fail. The International Organisation of Securities Commissions (IOSCO) and the Basel Committee on Payment and Settlement Systems (CPSS) are currently consulting on updated standards for CCPs to precisely that end.

If, nevertheless, a CCP does fail, the second component is a clear *ex ante* framework for limiting disorder. I fear that the international authorities have been playing catch-up on that endeavour, but it is now being pursued. It will involve providing clarity, ideally through the CCP's own rules, around the extent to which surviving clearing members are obliged to pick up the pieces, and a special resolution regime for when they cannot.[5]

Shadow banking

As we simplify the financial network with one hand, we need to take care not to complicate it with the other.

By redrawing the social contract for banking, international policymakers recognise that we are creating incentives for the riskier elements of banking – both commercial and investment banking – to be reinvented outside the banks. Society will be ill served if excessively risky structures threatening stability are constructed beyond the perimeter of prudential

supervision and of special resolution regimes. Of course, not all
non-bank structures are or need be unduly risky for the system
as a whole. We need a policy for those that are. This is driving
the international work on shadow banking.[6]

In the UK, the planned new regulatory architecture seeks to
cater for this by giving the Bank of England's new Financial
Policy Committee (FPC) an explicit responsibility for advising
the government when the perimeter of regulation should be
adjusted in some way. How we go about this will need to be
made transparent via the published record of our scheduled
quarterly meetings and the FPC's twice-yearly *Financial Stability
Reports*. This is part of the macroprudential endeavour.

Macroprudential regimes: taking a system-wide view

Alongside resolution, the great revolution in the rebuilding of
the regulatory regime for finance is, indeed, macroprudential
supervision and regulation.

This entails recovering the understanding of our predeces-
sors. Here is Sir George Blunden, the first chairman of the Basel
Committee, speaking in the mid-1980s, when he returned to
the Bank of England as deputy governor:[7]

> *Supervisory standards are set with an eye to protecting [banks] from
> problems which could be created by wider, systemic developments. A
> bank may consider a course of action it wishes to take to be acceptable
> – as it may well be in a limited context. But the same course might, if
> widely copied by other banks, have unfortunate effects on the banking
> system as a whole. It is part of the supervisors' job to take that wider,
> systemic view and sometimes to curb practices which even prudent
> banks might, if left to themselves, regard as safe.*

This can be unpacked into two insights, which have run

through this piece, and which imply a need for what these days are called 'macroprudential tools':

- the financial system is a system;
- any set of static requirements will eventually prove fatally flawed.

The two dimensions of macroprudential policy

It will not be possible to preserve the resilience of the financial system if we rely rigidly on a set of quantitative requirements for capital, liquidity and so on calibrated in 2010 − 11. Circumstances change. Booms in credit growth and asset prices − and, indeed, cumulative macroeconomic imbalances more generally − typically pose challenges to stability because as boom turns to bust, firms' financial resources get stretched. One important set of macroprudential tools involves temporarily varying requirements on balance-sheet structures or financing terms − such as minimum capital or minimum margin requirements − to reflect the increase in environmental risks. By taking away the punchbowl, we may well have the beneficial effect of dampening the boom itself. But, crucially, even if the boom were to persist, we would have put the system in a better position to absorb the bust without systemic distress. Even without direct management of the supply and allocation of credit, which in truth lies beyond our capability, we can shield the macroeconomy from credit crunches by making the financial system more resilient to stress as threats increase.

This is one dimension. There are two. As experience all too amply demonstrates, stress in the financial system is greater the more complex and opaque the network of exposures among firms and the less adequate a market's supporting (soft and hard) infrastructure. The international efforts on CCPs reviewed above are, of course, directed at just that. But it would be a mistake to think that current policymakers can envisage, let alone anticipate, all the issues we will face in future. A macro-prudential authority therefore needs a flexible range of tools, and to keep abreast of the evolution of the financial system. That has to include capital markets as well as banking.

The role of securities regulation in macroprudential policy

While banking supervisors are having to return to their roots, securities regulators are having to look well beyond their own roots. Their regimes for the issuance and distribution of secur-ities, for transparency, for trading platforms and for asset man-agement all matter greatly to the resilience of the financial system. This is beginning to be recognised. At a global level, IOSCO is represented on the FSB and, perhaps encouraged by that experience, in February 2011 it published an important report, *Mitigating Systemic Risk*.[8] In Europe, the European Secur-ities Markets Authority sits on the Systemic Risk Board. In the US, both the Commodity Futures Trading Commission and the Securities and Exchange Commission are on the new Financial Stability Oversight Council created by the Dodd-Frank legislation.

This is especially important for the UK. London's capital markets are so international that threats to stability from any corner of the globe ricochet through the system, and so through the economy. We cannot afford to ignore capital markets if we are to restore and preserve stability in the UK. The UK's new regime recognises this. The CEO of the planned new market regulator, the Financial Conduct Authority (FCA), will be a member of the FPC once it is placed on a statutory footing. And the government proposes that the FPC be given powers by Par-liament to give recommendations and directions to the FCA on where it could develop or apply its policies and rules in the interests of stability.

Summary: finance and the market economy

Market economies cannot operate without a stable financial system. I would go further. A market economy cannot succeed without a financial system that efficiently allocates capital to investment and development projects, and helps households ride the peaks and troughs in their lifetime income. A safe and sound banking sector is essential to that, and to an effective and efficient financial system more generally. Because of myopia about risk,[9] herding, asymmetric information and incentive issues, the state cannot leave finance entirely to its own devices. We are living through a period where millions of jobs have been lost and firms destroyed around the world because an enfeebled financial system could not absorb the crystallisation of risks from an overhang of debt, within and across countries. The 'rules of the game' for finance had failed to keep up with the progressive fusion of banking, capital markets and insurance; and they had not been 'flexed' in response to the accumulation of macroeconomic imbalances.

The greatest failure of all was the absence of a regime for the orderly resolution of distressed financial firms, without tax-payer solvency support.

The package emerging from the international community is just that — a package. Those of us who signed up to core capital requirements of around 10 per cent — or 13 per cent including convertibles — for the largest banks have done so in the light of other components of the package. Throughout this piece, I have stressed two. First, we are determined, and are on course, to put a credible resolution regime in place. This will ensure that, as well as equity holders, debt holders are exposed to loss. Wholesale creditors will then also have a powerful incentive to monitor the risks banks run, increasing market discipline. This is central to reincorporating banks into a market economy. Second, we are building macroprudential frameworks under which capital and other requirements can be adjusted temporarily — or 'counter-cyclically' — as and when risks are unusually high, and reduce them back to more 'normal' levels as extraordinary incipient threats recede. Those extra dimensions of the overall policy package have, rightly, mitigated the internationally required increases in equity capital.

It would be foolish to declare that policymakers know enough to get all this exactly right. We do not know enough about the existence of economies of scale and scope in large global banks and dealers. We do not know enough about how the incentives of asset managers investing in banks' equity and bonds affect the behaviour of banks. No one can know as much as we should like about the effects on the business cycle of introducing the existing package of reforms now — which is why we have tried to provide for extended transition periods. Some might argue that reform should wait until economic recovery is entrenched and until we have had time to do more research. But pursuing reform now is not just a matter of responding to public concern, important though this is. Credible reform is also crucial to restoring confidence in the financial system and thus to delivering a vibrant, effective system. This is necessary for durable economic recovery, and for sustainable economic growth over the longer term.

2

Where the G20 process went right and wrong

SHRITI VADERA

At the height of the financial crisis at the end of September 2008 the leaders of France, Germany and the UK persuaded a reluctant President George W. Bush to agree to the first G20 leaders' summit to boost confidence in the global economy. He agreed on two conditions: he would not have to travel to it; and they would ensure there would be some substance to which leaders could be seen to agree. He was somewhat indifferent to what that substance ought to be. It is perhaps not surprising that despite strong momentum and some achievements during 2009, the latest experiment in international coordination has largely lived down to its inauspicious start.

A good start

The fact that such a broad cross-section of world leaders could come together and agree on a common plan of action on fiscal and monetary measures, the provision of global liquidity and the reform of financial services meant that the world was able at that time to avoid the slide into protectionism and a depression that characterised the 1930s. It led some observers to claim to detect the dawn of a new era of international cooperation on reform, or even the advent of a new, expanded institution for global governance for a multi-polar world.

When the leaders gathered in Washington's colonnaded National Building Museum less than two months after deciding on a summit to discuss the global financial crisis, their words certainly did not lack ambition or a sense of urgency. They declared they would 'make sure that a global crisis, such as this one, does not happen again'. They promised to 'implement reforms that will strengthen financial markets and regulatory regimes so as to avoid future crises' with 'intensified international cooperation among regulators'.

Astonishingly to some, the declaration went on to set out 47 separate short- and medium-term action points designed to strengthen transparency, accountability and integrity in financial markets; enhance prudential oversight and risk management; and reform international institutions. And − a first for a leaders' summit − it had a timetable and process for reporting back on progress. A focus on implementation was a novel concept for those used over the years to the never-to-be-revisited declarations of a day from the G8. In a time of imminent danger, it was a moment of some hope.

Closer examination of the 47 action points reveals that they cover all the pet financial issues of individual governments, ranging from greater capital and living wills for the UK, leverage and liquidity ratios for the US, to the role of over-the-counter (OTC) derivatives, credit default swaps (CDS), credit-rating agencies and accounting standards for France. It was a laudable shopping list, not a coherent regulatory framework. What was missing was a sense of priorities and how the different action plans on everything from accounting standards to capital requirements to executive compensation were supposed to work together to reduce risk in the system. This was inevitable given that it had been the shortest possible lead time for an international summit, but it is a problem that has dogged the international coordination of financial services regulation ever since.

Basel III: a notable success

There have of course been crucial and notable successes, not least the 'un-American' Basel III accord agreed by the Basel Committee of Banking Supervision within two years, in time for the Seoul Summit in November 2010. On higher and better-quality capital requirements for banks, it is a significant improvement over its predecessor Basel II, which itself created some of the conditions that led to the financial crisis. For those who complain about the haste of this decision-making process, it should be clear from Basel II, ten years in the making, that in the world of international bureaucracy more time does not always mean better, more thought-through outcomes.

The requirements of the new regime included not only absolute capital ratios but also leverage ratios and liquidity standards, with significantly greater incentives to more appropriately assess and provide for risks. It does though continue to have some rather backward-looking risk assessments, such as risk-free weighting for highly rated sovereign debt, which would in other circumstances encourage banks to hold more euro-zone sovereign debt.

To judge by the cacophony of complaints from many in the banking industry — a test of effectiveness that spurs some regulators on — these are measures with real bite. Whatever disagreements individual banks may express with specific aspects of the rules, it would be hard for them to argue that the world would not have been a safer place had the more onerous regime of Basel III been in place, say, ten years ago. If the declared intention was, as stated, to prevent a rerun of 2008, then they now have in the capital regime a much better set of tools to help them.

The relative speed of the Basel III agreement is an important if rather singular success in the G20's coordination of financial regulation. It owes part of this success to the creation of the Financial Stability Board (FSB) at the London summit in April 2009. The FSB enlarged the membership of the long-standing but marginalised Financial Stability Forum, which had been appointed and dominated by the G7, to include all the members of the G20, thereby increasing its legitimacy.

The FSB was given a clear mandate on early warning of macroeconomic risks, the core tools of capital, liquidity and leverage, oversight of all systemically important financial institutions (SIFIs), including hedge funds for the first time, action on compensation, non-cooperative jurisdictions and credit-rating agencies. It was given authority in the only way the G20 grouping can, which is to mandate it in its communiqués to undertake a task and ask its consummately skilful chair at that time, Mario Draghi, to report back on progress to the G20 in person. G20 communiqués became littered with references to 'We call on the FSB to...'.

Despite insufficient resources and some early turf wars with the IMF, the FSB became an effective conduit for the political body of finance ministers and heads of government to demand urgent progress from the otherwise independent body of regulators of the Basel Committee. Indeed, if the FSB did not exist, we would need to invent it. However, the strength of its political patronage was also a weakness when the pressures of widely diverging political priorities on the G20 members became more apparent.

Political divergence

Bankers were not the only ones to complain about elements of Basel III. The view of German and French politicians from the start was that the crisis was just retribution being visited on the failed Anglo-Saxon model of unfettered markets. 'I want the world to see the victory of the European model, which has nothing to do with the excesses of financial capitalism,' declared President Nicolas Sarkozy at the time of Michel Barnier's appointment as commissioner for internal market and services in 2009.

Putting aside the inconvenient fact that more US subprime mortgages were owned by European banks and investors than were held in the US (at one stage $1.6 trillion compared with $1 trillion), major European banks went into the crisis generally better capitalised, less leveraged and hence more resilient than most US and UK banks. The French and Germans argued that requiring increased and purer forms of capital in all the world's banks was punishing everyone for poor regulation and supervision in the US and UK. They resisted the more onerous requirements in negotiations to the very end, and a hard-won concession was the delaying until 2019 of the final implementation date for Basel III.

Unfortunately, some European banks rode the cycle of the first phase of the crisis without any additional capitalisation and without adequately provisioning and working through their losses. So, with the tacit consent of their regulators, they came out of the turmoil of 2008 – 09 less resilient than many of their US and UK counterparts. Now that we are into the next sovereign phase of the crisis – and three European bank stress tests later – it shows an inherent weakness of internationally coordinated regulation. Banks are global, rules can be made universal, but implementation remains national.

It also remains politically influenced to a greater or lesser degree. Christine Lagarde, the new managing director of the IMF, made a timely and influential intervention in August 2011 to point out the need for European banks to increase capital. But since she had fought for the opposing French position on capital just months before, her statement shows that policymakers stand where they sit. In a world where banks are too interconnected to fail, not just too big to fail, national implementation requires a stringent mechanism of peer review between regulators to ensure the new rules will really be effective.

Continental European countries did not come under the same pressure to reform their banking systems, as they blamed the crisis on developments abroad. Their focus instead remained on using European regulation and international coordination to curb elements of what President Sarkozy declared the 'all-powerful market without any rules' − shorting, OTC, CDS, hedge funds, bankers' compensation, mark to market valuation and non-cooperative jurisdictions to name but a few.

For the US, UK and a few other countries, a different political pressure prevailed to get tough with their banks, especially those seen as too big to fail. In the crucial areas of capital, leverage and liquidity, a race to the bottom where countries seek competitive advantage through more lax standards had been avoided. However, myriad 'Swiss finish' national options to supplement these measures have not. The US authorities have been the most explicit in their view that while coordination for the minimum standards was all well and good, each country was entitled to implement individual higher standards to meet its specific financial (and political) needs.

This rationalisation was of course expressed retrospectively after the furious reaction from some G20 regulators caught on the hop by President Barack Obama's announcement of his support for the 'Volcker Rule' in January 2010, which seeks to ban large US banks from trading on their own account and to impose strict limits on banks' ownership of hedge funds. Legislators incorporated this rule into the Dodd-Frank Wall Street Reform and Consumer Protection Act, and regulators are now tying themselves in knots trying to turn a broad prescription into a detailed policy.

The timing of the original announcement, and possibly the content, was driven by election-year calculations. It came, in fact, at the exact time when the FSB was in session and discussing responses to the very issue of SIFIs, of which a significant number would be from the US. The announcement was news to the Americans at the session too. It was a body blow to the enthusiasm and effort vested in international regulatory coordination beyond Basel III.

Too interconnected to fail

This issue of the big global banks, with assets in some cases many times larger than the GDP of the countries where they were based, was at the heart of the original problem and now is at the heart of regulatory incoherence. There would be no disagreement that the approach should be to prevent failure as far as possible; minimise the cost to taxpayers in the event of an inevitable failure; ensure an orderly resolution, especially across borders, which reduces the overall risk of contagion; and so credibly allow the failure and hence remove the taxpayers' implicit subsidy and the moral hazard for inappropriate risk-taking. The theory is rather different from the implementation.

In the UK, there was the Vickers Commission, one of whose main recommendations was to set up a ring fence between a banking group's retail activities, subject to government-mandated deposit protection, and its separately capitalised investment banking business. It is driven by an understandable desire to protect the UK taxpayer in the event of future bank failures, even if its origins were more political in the then UK opposition's desire to show it would be tougher than the government in dealing with banks.

So in two important jurisdictions, banks are being asked to create different forms of separation between various parts of their business to curb and protect against some of the banks' riskier activities, while Europe focuses on promoting a financial transactions tax and the UK extends its bank levy, and the Basel Committee has required additional loss-absorbing capital to be carried by the largest SIFIs. Regardless of the merits of these individual approaches, their coexistence, together with the multiple other ways in which national authorities are pulling in different directions, is likely to complicate the task of supervising SIFIs immeasurably. It remains a legitimate question whether in aggregate the complexity of these multiple approaches makes the global system safer.

Most critically, as the Basel Committee acknowledged in July 2011 in one of its more diplomatically damning assessments, insufficient progress is being made on the commitment to create a cross-border resolution regime that would allow failed global banks to be wound up with minimal disruption to markets. Not all countries even have effective national resolution regimes. The UK and US have arrangements in place that can probably cope quite well with the collapse of a small domestic bank, but the same cannot be said for the failure of a large cross-border bank. Where national regimes exist, they show no signs of convergence or mutual recognition as promised and little ability to deal with cross-border complexities, particularly those that would allow continuation of critical functions through temporary 'bridge banks' or bail-in powers. Further work is awaited in 2012 but progress appears painfully slow.

It raises the question of what would happen if a large and complex global banking group of systemic importance in multiple jurisdictions were to get into difficulty in the near future. In the event of another 'Lehman moment', it is possible that the market chaos could be every bit as severe and the authorities every bit as impotent as they were then.

Regulatory market

Regulatory incoherence in some areas is matched with regulatory neglect or worryingly slow progress in others, particularly macroprudential regulation and the needs of emerging markets where issues are difficult or simply not considered important in the short term. Macroprudential regulation has been mentioned with little impact in almost every G20 communiqué.

Its accepted importance is based on the view that the consideration of system-wide risks fell between two stools: the exclusive focus by central banks on price stability, and the exclusive focus of bank regulators on firm-level supervision and regulation (micro-prudential policy). The objective is to spot and prick asset bubbles before they pose a systemic risk. A wider global early-warning system could also have more vociferously warned of the inevitable sovereign crises that follow bank crises. It is not a task that economic history suggests has met with resounding success. Indeed, until fairly recently the whole idea was dismissed by some important central bankers as impossible or preposterous.

It is an area where there has been relatively little published academic research and there are few established conventions, and it is perhaps therefore unsurprising that it is in the 'too difficult' category. While it is regarded as an essential ingredient in the policy mix, attempts to put anything into practice at even national level are in their infancy. There appears insufficient consensus about its precise objectives and what might constitute an effective toolkit for identification and mitigation of risks.

One important area needing focus to avoid future crises of the scale recently experienced is reducing the pro-cyclical influence of the banking system. Counter-cyclical capital buffers may be inadequate as a response on their own. The G20 leaders called in Washington for immediate 'recommendations to mitigate pro-cyclicality, including the review of how valuation and leverage, bank capital, executive compensation, and provisioning practices may exacerbate cyclical trends'. Any action in agreeing an international approach, however, should not ignore the complexities arising from the huge differences between one country's banking system and economic cycle and another's.

A further area in which the G20 process has not delivered what it originally promised is the needs of emerging markets. While including a wider range of participants from China, India, South Africa, Brazil and countries outside the G20 in deliberations on financial reform was potentially a big step forward in process, it has yet to translate into a step forward in outcomes.

Trade finance, of primary importance to emerging markets, carries disproportionate regulatory cost — greater than its underlying economic cost. The role of subsidiaries in emerging markets was ignored for a long period during the debate on SIFIs. Emerging markets fear that while they are still at a stage where they need to develop financial intermediation in their economies, global regulatory rules are being targeted exclusively at curbing activities. And they fear the cost of increased regulation will be passed on disproportionately to their borrowers because it is easier to do that in a relatively underdeveloped market.

Emerging markets have been voicing increasing frustration that their specific concerns are not being addressed. It sometimes seems to them as if they are still expected to sit as silent witnesses to an esoteric debate among their apparently more mature peers about issues that do not concern them. This complaint was officially acknowledged at the G20's Seoul summit in November 2010, whose final communiqué pointedly promised to 'better reflect the perspective of emerging market economies in financial regulatory reforms'.

Governments that feel their concerns have not been addressed in a negotiation are by definition less likely to have a stake in the outcome and less likely to be rigorous about implementing the resulting decisions. That makes regulatory arbitrage, say, between the mature markets of North America and Europe and the rapidly growing economies of Asia more likely. To take this thought to its logical conclusion: who knows where the next global banking crisis is likely to originate? The biggest banks in the world are no longer just American or European but also Asian. To solve the crisis of the future and not just lock the stable door on the past, global regulatory rules have to take account of the needs of emerging markets.

Conclusion

While the international score card is held up by the cornerstone achievement of Basel III, much of the remainder is a confusing and overlapping patchwork of nationally or regionally driven regulatory efforts interspersed with unaddressed risks seemingly too difficult to deal with. The cumulative impact in terms of both effectiveness against the stated objectives of system safety and the cost/benefit ratio remains unknown but suspect. Nevertheless, the prospectus for global regulatory cooperation and reform set out by the early G20 communiqués remains a work in progress that deserves maximum political support at the highest level around the world. Any political leader who has been through the travails of the past few years of financial crisis will have no desire to repeat the experience, and global regulatory reform is still the essential preventive medicine.

That international cooperation has been imperfect is a reflection of the contradictory world of democratic politics. Politicians want the system to be safer but still to provide ever-expanding credit at affordable cost. They want a better-regulated financial sector but also to compete for business in a globalised world. They do not like excessive compensation for bankers but love the income-tax revenues it generates. They want effective measures that deal with complex financial institutions but need simple headlines that easily grab public imagination. Above all, they recognise the role of international coordination and compromise but their voters are at home.

While we should not be surprised if they fumble in their execution of unpalatable choices, we should demand perseverance in the path that was charted in the 2008 and 2009 G20 summits. The G20 is an uncomfortable forum where politics meets finance and economics. It cannot create consensus where none exists, but true leadership can. That consensus was stronger during the height of the crisis because leaders understood instinctively the words of Thomas Paine: 'If we do not hang together, we shall surely hang separately.' That sense of common cause has faded with the memory of collective near-death experience.

The memory of bankers has proven even shorter. Legitimate concerns about the effectiveness of measures masquerade under attempts to return to the old normal of high risks and high rewards. The unedifying stampede back to 'business as usual' in 2009 – 10 demonstrates the remarkable ability of many smart people to ignore the obvious. More capital, less risk, lower returns, lower compensation: these are the demands from society and the global economy, which was nearly brought to its knees as recently as 2008 by their catastrophic miscalculation of risk. We are still hearing howls of protest from some quarters about the excessive regulatory burden and the allegedly misguided nature of many of the new requirements.

Perhaps if nothing else the protests serve to indicate that the regulators are beginning to get a grip, and that is as it should be.

3

Risk in financial institutions – is it managed?

EDDY WYMEERSCH

Although the banking crisis of the latter half of 2011 can be attributed to the legacy of the years 2007–09, new flaws have appeared, leading to serious concerns about the overall concept of today's banking business.[1] Specific incidents like the discovery of rogue trading, causing undeniable damage to the system and its credibility, along with continuous concerns about mis-selling, both on the asset side and with respect to investment products, cause considerable damage to the reputation of the financial sector as a whole. This reflection on the way banks handle their risks, and how risk management relates to their overall governance structure, aims to give an overview of the state of the art these days, with some recommendations for future strengthening.

The subject of risk management has been extensively analysed and discussed by national, European and international banking authorities,[2] all calling for a stricter risk-oversight structure, more elaborate and detailed procedures, and finer analytical work. Private organisations have analysed in great

detail the techniques of appropriate risk management as prac-
tised today in large banks. All this has led to a new perception
where 'risk' is the name of the game.

Risk awareness

Looking back to pre-crisis times, one of the striking evolutions
over the last few years is undoubtedly the increasing interest in
risk management. Issues that were at the forefront of discussions before 2008, such as financial conglomerates, Basel II
implementation or shareholder value, have not faded but are
overwhelmed by the focus on risk issues. This is clearly reflected
in the increasing number of statements, recommendations,
legislative proposals and other initiatives dealing with risk in
its multifarious aspects. The number of bodies that have 'risk'
at the top of their agenda is impressive: the IMF, World Bank,
Bank for International Settlements (BIS), Basel Committee on
Banking Supervision (BCBS), European Commission and Committee of European Banking Supervisors (CEBS) — now the
European Banking Authority (EBA) — have laid the ground-
work for a comprehensive if not always well coordinated drive
for radically improving risk techniques, procedures or internal
structures. There are also, at the more practical level, the statements of the Senior Supervisors Group (SSG) and the numerous
detailed 'guidance notes' on risk-management organisation
published by national supervisory authorities. And on the
industry side, there are the reports and publications of the
Institute of International Finance (IIF), a global association of
financial institutions, including the world's major banks. The
implementation of many of these new recommendations is
still under way, and although significant progress has been
made in the banks' internal rules, the actual roll-out will still
require further time, effort and budgetary expenditures.

Looking at these numerous reports, statements,

recommendations, codes of conduct and guidance, the conclusion must be that the risk issue has now become central to all developments in the banking sector.[3] This concern has partially been taken up by the markets as well: some of the riskiest pre-crisis products have more or less disappeared, such as securitisation, collateralised debt obligations (CDOs) and other synthetic products. Furthermore, risk-measurement tools have been improved, for instance in the form of risk indices, or even as credit default swaps (CDSs). As a result there is more risk awareness, which should contribute to lowering the risk profile of financial institutions.

At the same time, risk in financial institutions changed from a risk profile based on the analysis of the individual institution to overall or macro risk analysis, as financial stability, or even as systemic risk. Risk is no longer perceived as the risk of the individual institution, but includes an overarching risk factor that may affect several institutions or even the financial system as a whole. This change in perspective is reflected in a change in terminology from 'prudential supervision' to 'macro-prudential supervision'. This took place in the early 2000s and led to a significant overhaul in the structure of financial supervision, putting central banks at the centre of the supervisory network. Today, systemic concerns dominate in banking regulation as well as in the areas of alternative investment funds, market organisation, exchange-traded funds, and so on. To cope with this new challenge, new institutions dealing with systemic risk and overall financial stability have been created to address the aggregate situation of individual financial institutions, especially the linkages between them and the other factors that may trigger risk contagion among otherwise independent legal entities.[4]

The drive to reposition the banking system as a major and in several respects systemic risk bearer raises the question of whether this evolution leaves sufficient room for the traditional business functions of banks: that is, the distribution of credit and organisation of payment systems. Although the excesses of the past cannot be excused, it is important to be aware that excessive regulatory caution may hamper economic recovery and even put in danger the banks' ability to recover from past and still undigested losses. Here the best may be the enemy of the good.

Accompanying this evolution is a fear that most of the activity that banks now refrain from undertaking will move to other, less regulated sectors. This is often referred to as 'shadow banking', a wholesale term covering a wide diversity of financial and quasi-financial firms.

Although not all financial activity should be covered by the same rules, there is clearly a need for an all-encompassing regime of oversight that will recognise developments in sectors that are usually not covered by traditional prudential regulation. The principle should be that no financial activity escapes the sharp eyes of the financial supervisors. Alternative investment funds are often cited in this context: as far as Europe is concerned, the recently adopted Directive on Alternative Investment Fund Managers should contain sufficiently detailed instruments to deal with risk developments up to the level of systemic concerns.

Broadening this view to developments outside the financial sector, risk management in non-financial firms is equally important and may have consequences that are just as devastating.

The role of the board in risk management

It is now widely accepted that the board has an active role to play in overseeing and monitoring the risk-management structure within a bank or financial institution. On the one hand, the board should require management to propose an appropriate and efficient risk-management policy, including the development of a risk-appetite framework to identify risks on a firm-wide basis and by business line. On the other hand, it should mandate the introduction of supporting IT schemes that will allow senior management and the board to gain timely and comprehensive insight into the risk position adopted at any given moment and on an evolving basis by each of the business lines, thus permitting corrections where necessary. On the basis of this overall insight, strategic decisions can be made.

At the overall organisation level, the European Union's proposed Capital Requirements Directive (CRD4) reiterates these organisational duties[5] and requires a bank's board to constitute within its ranks a risk committee, thereby formally embedding the risk approach in the bank's overall governance.[6] Although several larger banks have already instituted a risk committee, or a risk and capital committee, the rule will now be applicable to all banks, although smaller institutions can retain the function within the board itself without setting up a separate formal committee. The risk committee is composed of non-executive directors and high levels of technical expertise are required. Committee members should have a good knowledge of risk strategy and be capable of judging the firm's risk appetite.

The risk committee acts as an expert advisory body to the board, essentially ensuring that developments in the risk-appetite framework are followed up, but the board makes the final decisions. This applies particularly in cases where the board has to decide on certain derogations from risk limits, or their transfer from one business line to another. The risk committee should establish a close dialogue with, and encourage dialogue among, the senior managers responsible for risk matters: the chief executive officer (CEO), the chief financial officer (CFO) and the chief risk officer (CRO).

The committee is expected to oversee the introduction of a robust risk culture within the bank. This involves setting up a risk function: a vertical risk line established throughout the entire organisation. The directive also mandates the designation chief risk officer (CRO),[7] defining the person's status and position within the firm, and the introduction of procedures and guidelines for making the business lines and their leaders aware of the risk framework. It requires management to develop the necessary IT tools and data collection that will allow it to capture risk developments, both within the firm and in the markets, and to determine the firm's risk appetite, one of the core concepts in today's approach to risk.

In these new developments the concept of 'risk appetite' plays a crucial rule. It has been defined as 'the amount and type of risk that a company is able and willing to accept in pursuit of its business objectives', taking into account the desired returns. It is to be distinguished from 'risk capacity' as this is the amount of risk a firm is willing — and able — to support given its capital, liquidity, and so on, but also taking into account losses and negative events that can reasonably be calculated. According to the definition, risk appetite should not exceed risk capacity, and if that does occur, the necessary adjustments will have to be made, either by lowering the risk position or by increasing the risk capacity. Risk appetite also indicates the way a firm wants to be seen by its different stakeholders, including its employees, the regulators and the rating agencies.

Defining risk appetite is complex, being more of a learning curve in which the different players will become better acquainted with the sometimes intricate risk positions and the equally complex ways to mitigate those risks.[8] Its validity is verified in stress tests carried out after the event. This is a complex exercise that has also been described as more of a learning process than a firm or rigid determination of risks.

A risk policy requires the risks to be identified, assessed and evaluated throughout the organisation, and also calls for a follow-up in terms of monitoring the business lines. Although essentially implemented from a risk perspective, it can be a powerful driver for unlocking value by encouraging a better alignment between decision-making and risk. Both activities are within the remit of the risk-management line that cuts across the entire organisation and that, although remaining in close dialogue with the operational staff, ultimately reports to the CRO.

The risk officers or oversight staff, who are part of management, determine the risk centres, identify the probability and volume of the risk, and prepare the risk appetite statement; in some instances they may be entitled to intervene in business operations on the basis of risk considerations, although this point is somewhat controversial.[9] They should also be able to act independently and not be subject to the instructions of department heads. The risk policy should cover the entire organisation and include all subsidiaries, at least those that are consolidated in the accounts. The risk-oversight staff should have access to all information within the organisation, and be able to collect the necessary information from the operational staff and draw up risk charts that will feed into the risk-appetite statement. For all these reasons the risk officers' legal and functional position has to be defined by the board.

The breadth of their tasks and their sometimes difficult relationship with the operational line managers raise the issue of the legal and actual position of risk officers, especially the CRO, in the management of the bank. The CRO's position is a balancing act between action and control. He will normally be of a sufficiently high rank,[10] probably a member of the executive,[11] or at least taking part in the meetings of the executive body and contributing to its significant strategic decisions, but sufficiently independent so that he can criticise decisions of that body without being fully subject to the views of the CEO or the executive. This means that his appointment, or at least his dismissal, should take place with the board's agreement, or in the case of his resignation the board should be adequately informed.[12] However, he should have a direct reporting line to the risk committee, which can ask him to present reports on specific items. But he remains part of the executive, ensuring that his staff have permanent access to the leaders of the business lines.

The risk policy also has an influence on the labour relations and remuneration policy, which should be consistent with effective risk management and not encourage risk-taking that exceeds the level of tolerated risk.[13] Apart from the remuneration debate at the senior management level, some firms link promotion and compensation to adherence to the risk-appetite framework.[14]

Banks' governance and macro risks

In principle, banks as corporate entities are subject to the general corporate law and governance rules, which vary depending on whether their shares are traded on the public stock markets or not. This regime can be considered a default regime, as banks and financial institutions must adhere to much more demanding standards in terms of good governance because they play an important part in public confidence and may create considerable negative externalities for depositors, creditors and society at large. Some decisions may trigger wider risks, usually referred to as contagion risks, which may become systemic risks. This is often considered to affect only the largest financial institutions, and especially the systemically important financial institutions (SIFIs). Contagion can develop from small events that shake market confidence, such as suspension or reimbursement of investment fund shares, or that disrupt the regular function of trading in a market, like the so-called 'flash crash' on US stock markets on 6 May 2010. Most larger banks or financial firms should ask themselves whether and how their actions could lead to significant contagion, and hence to systemic developments.

Reformulating the question in terms of corporate governance, this would mean that boards of directors would have to ask themselves whether their decisions – and worse, their non-decisions – would affect these wider, often unfathomable risks, and consequently adapt those decisions, if needed, subordinating their direct financial interest to the public interest.

In theory and according to traditional analysis, private companies are not accountable to the public interest: they serve only the interests of their investors – shareholders and creditors – and their other stakeholders. Identifying what is in the public interest and how this is to be achieved is the task of public authorities, legislators or regulators. If firms have to respect certain rules of general interest, these should be imposed by law or regulation. In reality, matters are not that simple.

To what extent should firms include these wider – especially contagion – risks in their internal decision-making? Could a firm and its directors be held accountable for having taken decisions that were manifestly detrimental to the financial system as a whole, or to a country's treasury? The answer is usually negative, as the nature of this obligation will be too indeterminate, and the bank's board or management would first have to honour its duties – including fiduciary duties – towards its investors and shareholders. Only in view of clear and legally based instructions from state bodies would the answer be different.

Beyond a strict legal analysis, however, a bank may take into account its wider responsibility to the community within which it operates. The balance will be difficult: can a bank in a crisis withdraw foreign exchange from its subsidiaries abroad, creating difficulties for the host state? And what about shorting the host state's bonds to protect a bank's own assets? In the longer term, a bank may need to take account of these wider interests to safeguard and protect its reputation and standing in its host community.

The proposal for a new Capital Requirements Directive (CRD4) in its Article 75 § 1 seems to include the follow-up of some macro risks in the overall description of the board's tasks, where it states:

> *Competent authorities shall ensure that the management body*
> *approves and periodically reviews the strategies and policies for*
> *taking up, managing, monitoring and mitigating the risks the*
> *institution is or might be exposed to, including those posed by the*
> *macroeconomic environment in which it operates in relation to the*
> *status of the business cycle.*

This reference to the business cycle could be read as relating to the pro-cyclicality measures that are alluded to in other provisions of the directive, but it does not clearly require banks to take responsibility for the externalities that may be caused by macro events.

In the absence of a clear legal position, the link between macroprudential policy and bank management needs further analysis. Public authorities are in the process of developing tools for identifying negative developments in the field of systemic risk. In Europe, the recently instituted European Systemic Risk Board (ESRB) is in charge of identifying these risks and will, if needed, issue recommendations and warnings. These are addressed to the European Supervisory Authorities (ESAs), which should then transmit the information to their members, the national supervisory authorities. It is unclear to what extent the latter authorities can require banks or financial institutions to adhere to these policies other than by explicit regulatory or prudential measures, for which often there will be no legal basis.

A certain number of tools exist already and have been deployed by governments in many jurisdictions. These include adapting loan-to-value ratios, reducing exposure limits, imposing transaction taxes, restricting certain risky products, prohibiting certain foreign-currency borrowing, strengthening lending criteria, and ultimately bolstering provisions and capital.[15] Although most of these instruments have been introduced for objectives other than macroprudential ones, such as consumer protection, market stability or creating tax revenues, they have undeniable effects on financial stability and risk reduction. These measures should all be based on explicit legal foundations and cannot be subsumed into the bank's generally formulated business strategy. Apart from these explicit measures, recommendations for other measures that are not provided for in the regulation may be needed. Given the prominent position of the Financial Stability Board, financial institutions would be well advised to heed its recommendations, even if these are not legally binding.

Risk-management tools: risk appetite

Developing a risk-appetite framework is not simple: introducing an all-pervasive awareness of risk, in sharp contrast to the previously pursued objective of return on assets, can be a bit of a culture shock. The exercise involves the entire firm but allows for some diversity in specific businesses. Being largely based on quantitative models, resulting in limits that are familiar to or at least easily understood by staff, it also incorporates qualitative elements or unquantifiable risks that are more difficult to explain or justify. Operational staff should be closely involved in the exercise, as they must understand the reasons and accept the need for the restrictions, not least because this may directly affect their financial position. Moreover, the exercise is expensive and time-consuming and may require a lot of innovative brainwork. It is essential to recognise that the exercise will not succeed if it is not strongly supported by the entire organisation, including the board, top management and the heads of the business lines, who must explain the framework and convince their staff that it is necessary. In short, it must become part of the firm's overall culture.

There is no single methodology for measuring a bank or financial institution's risk appetite. Even within a group there may be differences, although these should have some overall consistency. Nestor Advisors, a UK consultancy, identified two methodologies: the first is essentially quantitative in terms of strategic guidance based on a classical risk–return trade-off; the second is based on quantitative elements fixing boundaries for acceptable risk. The qualitative method used by big French banks, among others, gives little guidance to risk takers and may expose a bank to bottom-up pressures. The simplest methods essentially set targets for the different risk categories, and may be complemented by qualitative measures such as reputation, compliance with regulation and management motivation. The more elaborate qualitative instruments are usually based on financial targets, such as capital, rating, earnings volatility, liquidity ratio and regulatory standing.[16] Economic capital is used as a measure for determining the capital needs for different levels of unexpected events — stress testing and scenario analyses are used in this approach. For some segments of banks' activities, such as exposure to credit risk, figures are already published. Other methods, such as value at risk (VaR), are frequently used and should be applied with the usual caveats.

This exercise results in a formal risk-appetite statement that is put forward by the executive board, the highlights of which are submitted to the main board for final approval. It establishes the boundaries fixed by the board within which the different departments can act, given the proposed strategy. The risk-appetite statement is not normally published, although some annual reports give detailed information on risk management.

A few essential guidelines should be followed when using risk appetite as a management tool. There should be a good understanding of the objectives of the exercise, which should not be considered final and is always open to review, refinements and new methods. Risk appetite is part of and should be closely linked to a company's strategy and financial planning. Beware a mathematical approach: formal limits give a misleading impression of safety and exclude further discussion. Contingency measures are necessary and escalation has to be provided for.

Beyond these technical aspects, the board should have a good general understanding of the risks involved in a financial institution's overall business. Some aspects have been spelled out in generally accepted statements of the prudential regulatory authorities such as the Basel Committee. Although these statements are essentially for the management, the board, which bears the ultimate responsibility, should remain vigilant. An example is the 'know your structure' rule. The board should have a clear understanding of the structure of the group of companies that form the financial institution. Although some complexity cannot be avoided, it should be a concern if the group structure has become so complex that it is opaque, leaving pockets of risk in invisible or impenetrable areas. Special attention should be given to important unconsolidated subsidiaries, as was illustrated in the CDO crisis. This point will require more attention once the practice of introducing 'living wills' enabling regulators to wind down failed banks has become more widespread.

'Know your customer' is another maxim of prudent banking, essentially addressed to the management. But a vigilant board cannot be insensitive to the regulatory reputation risk that may arise from doing business with undesirable clients.

Types of risks

Dealing with risk is the primary task of any bank or financial institution. It should develop appropriate policies and strategies for identifying, managing, mitigating and monitoring risks — always under the attentive eye of a supervisor.

Most types of risk have been identified and mitigation and evaluation methods are widely known.[17] The proposed Capital Requirements Directive contains a list of different types of risk, stating for several of them some additional requirements. This list is not considered to be conclusive, as new types of risk are likely to appear over time. Some types of risk are not specifically mentioned but are considered to be included in the widely defined categories. For example, there is no mention of reputation risk or systemic risk as such, as these are seen as incremental phases in existing types of risk; IT risk and legal risk would normally qualify under the general heading of operational risk, but will have to be considered separately as part of the overall risk-determination process.

A short overview of the approach of the proposed directive illustrates the concerns at the time of drafting:

- Credit and counterparty risk.[18] Credit institutions are urged to assess these risks — including default and migration risk — themselves and develop internal ratings-based approaches rather than relying exclusively on credit ratings.[19]
- Residual risk, relating to the existing methodologies and techniques that may be flawed.[20] This might include tail risk.

- Concentration risk, for which written policies and procedures are required but no overall figure is mentioned.[21]
- Securitisation risk, including reputation risk and provision of liquidity plans for amortisations.[22]
- Market risk, where attention is drawn to risks of a shortage of liquidity for short transactions.
- Interest risk arising from non-trading book activities.[23]
- Operational risks with special attention to low-frequency high-severity events, and reference to contingency and business continuity plans.[24] Key risk indicators alert managers to impending problems, allowing them to take mitigating action. Often these risks are unpredictable and not quantifiable, for example legal risk and reputational risk. Mitigation through insurance has been mentioned.
- Liquidity risk has received detailed attention. Institutions should communicate risk tolerance to all relevant business lines and countries where business is conducted.
- Risk of excessive leverage, referring to the leverage ratio determined in accordance with Article 416 of the CRD.[25]

Legal risk has not been well explored and deserves more attention. It is difficult to recognise before the event and may show up many years later, after the courts have handed down their final decision, and often a long time after the board members and managers involved have left. The causes can be subtle (nullity of contracts, unsatisfactory disclosure, biased advice) but the consequences can be destructive for the institution and may even become systemic.[26]

Some risks are rarely discussed, such as the risk from shareholders or from group structures. Obviously the rating of a financial institution can affect its owners, but the opposite may also occur, for example if a shareholder (such as a sovereign state) has its rating downgraded or becomes insolvent, putting the institution into play. Reputation damage or conflicts of interest may also affect an institution's reliability, especially in countries where relations with shareholders are opaque, or where dominant shareholders use their position to gain considerable private benefits of control.[27]

Involving auditors

It is striking that in the debate on risk management the intervention of auditors is rarely mentioned. This is because developing a risk policy is essentially an internal management matter, aimed at steering and alerting managers, and not one of external communication, which is the outcome of an auditor's activity. However, many of the assessments in the risk-appetite framework are highly relevant to an auditor's analysis of valuations and risks; therefore the auditor should at least have access to the reports and findings developed as part of the framework. The Senior Supervisors Group, in its original report, drew attention to the need to involve auditors without clarifying to what extent and in what way they should be involved. It is undeniable that more attention has to be paid to fraud and illegal conduct, in serious cases to be reported to the supervisors.

When auditors use the data relating to an audited institution, according to International Auditing Standards (ISAs), they should first 'perform risk assessment procedures to provide a basis for the identification and assessment of risks of material misstatement at the financial statement and assertion level'.[28] This is an essential step in guaranteeing the integrity and reliability of the published data.

Involving shareholders

It is equally striking that there is little or no reference to shareholders, although in discussions on corporate governance they are the centre of attention. Once again, this is because risk management is essentially seen as a management issue, with managers acting under the overall oversight of the board. But this does not mean that shareholders underestimate the importance of risk management, and the annual reports of financial institutions – at least the best ones – do pay considerable attention to the issue.

It would help in the analysis to differentiate based on ownership structure. In small banks, mostly with concentrated ownership, the controlling shareholder generally keeps a close eye on the risk evolution of the organisation. But most large banks, mainly because of their high capital requirements, have a dispersed ownership structure in which shareholders have a limited role, their oversight being essentially exercised through the members of the board. Therefore the selection of candidates for board positions is crucial, and those responsible should strive to identify candidates who, as non-executives, are 'sufficiently knowledgeable and have the necessary skills and expertise to understand the risk strategy and the risk appetite'.[29] This applies to all members of the risk committee, and it may be hard to find people with sufficient technical insight and expertise in the firm's overall environment – only former bankers may qualify. Questions may arise with respect to former officers of a bank, as they could be biased when making decisions on issues in which they were previously involved. The proposed directive requires only that the members of the risk committee should be non-executive, not that they should be independent.

Shareholders are informed about an institution's principal risks in its annual report. When a company is using financial instruments, the financial risk management objectives and policies, and its exposure to price risk, credit and liquidity risk, and cash-flow risk, must be included in the annual report.[30] For listed companies, this is done pursuant to Article 46 of the

European Council's 4th Companies Directive and national regulations. A listed company's annual report should contain a description of the main features of its internal control and risk-management systems in relation to the financial reporting process.[31] The CEBS (now the EBA) guidelines on consolidated financial reporting do not contain a specific reference to this point.[32]

Conclusion

Developing an elaborate risk-management function, especially one with a focus on risk appetite, is still a fairly recent phenomenon. Implementation in banks and financial institutions is still under way and is likely to take time and a considerable investment in IT. Where things stand in the process of introducing a reliable risk appetite framework depends on the source of information. In December 2010, the Senior Supervisors Group stated that significant progress had been made in 'conceptualising, articulating and implementing a risk appetite framework' but that these improvements left some doubt about whether 'firms will have advanced these practices sufficiently to be resilient in an increasingly competitive and changing regulatory environment'. The SSG identified the task of aggregating risk data as the main challenge ahead.[33] The industry itself has a more positive view, recognising that more work remains to be done but citing figures illustrating that about 80 per cent of large banks have taken the necessary measures. The remaining hurdles, according to this view, are 'organisational silos, decentralisation of resources and decision-making, lack of integrated data management and delivery, and inherent complexities of operating globally'.[34]

4

The impact of regulation on remuneration

TOM GOSLING

Remuneration has been one of the most high-profile and comment-worthy fields of regulatory intervention over the past two years. But a survey carried out by Pricewaterhouse-Coopers (PwC) in 2008 found that only 13 per cent of respondents at financial services firms felt that regulation would be a major force for change in remuneration practices. The reality has turned out somewhat differently — regulators can claim, with some justification, that they have had a major impact on remuneration within the banking industry in recent years.

Forces for change

Regulators, although moving at different speeds, are largely aligned in recognising remuneration as an important issue of relevance to financial stability. And we have seen active dialogue on the issue, in large part through the auspices of the Financial Stability Board (FSB) and the G20.

Economics also has its role to play. As banks have grappled with impairment losses and higher capital requirements, levels of return on equity that were once considered normal have now become aspirational. So firms have had to work harder to make sure they are getting value for money from compensation. There has been an increased use of deferral programmes and the search for innovative deferral instruments, significantly driven by capital and cost pressures.

An international challenge?

But as regulation has developed, the fragile international consensus on reform has started to fracture. Within the G20 very different approaches have been taken: from the rules-based approach in Europe implemented through the Capital Requirements Directives (CRD3), through the principles-led firm-by-firm approach in the US, to almost nothing at all in some territories. The reaction of these last territories is that the issue has never really affected them and so they have taken a less zealous approach to adopting regulation.

The lack of a level playing field could hamper efforts for continued reform. But the common elements globally are sufficient for the industry to be convinced that change will be enduring. Common themes are finding their way into the Basel III texts on remuneration and are starting to apply to all sectors of financial services through the European directives (for example, through the emerging developments in relation to Solvency II).

What are the main issues to consider?

Central to the regulations is the need for banks to demonstrate to regulators that remuneration is structured so as not to encourage excessive risk-taking. The three pillars that have emerged through the financial crisis are as follows:

- *Remuneration governance.* What changes are required to the governance of remuneration to make sure conflicts of interest are managed, and alignment with the firm's risk appetite can be demonstrated?
- *Design of compensation.* How should compensation be used to ensure executives' risk-taking is appropriate?
- *Incorporation of risk into performance measures.* How can management ensure that bonus outcomes adequately capture the risk assumed in generating profits in a given year?

So what has been achieved and what remains to be done?

Remuneration governance

Perhaps the most profound changes to come out of the current crisis will be changes to governance arrangements, extending beyond pay. But governance in relation to pay is important in its own right. This is partly because the way that pay systems are governed influences behaviour as much as the technical design of incentives, but also because the way a firm is governed in relation to pay can be a visible signal of how its governance operates more widely.

Regulators now require some kind of annual report on remuneration practices throughout the firm. This may even extend to certification from the remuneration committee's chairman that the policies discourage excessive risk-taking and are robustly enforced. At major banks an annual interview of the chairmen of the remuneration committee will form part of the process.

These developments represent a significant extension of the remit of remuneration committees. Consideration should be given to how the type of certification likely to be needed will be supported. This requires a wider review of the governance arrangements covering pay.

Figure 4.1 **Remuneration committee: changes in relationships**

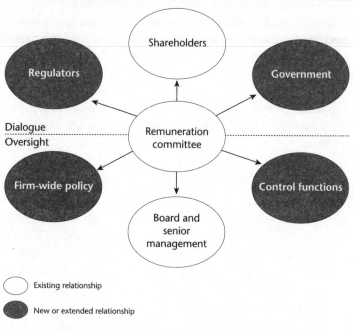

The traditional role of the remuneration committee has been to oversee the remuneration of the most senior executives, with reporting accountability to shareholders through the remuneration report. This has typically involved a view of broader remuneration policy, but in practice this diminishes rapidly below executive committee level.

There are now two significant potential changes to this remit. Both regulators and governments (for banks receiving state aid) are now potential stakeholders in relation to remuneration practices. Both are likely to have reporting requirements. The interest of these stakeholders extends beyond the traditional shareholder interest in executive director remuneration and into remuneration policy across the firm.

Boards need to consider whether the remuneration committee as it currently stands can effectively fulfil, and be demonstrated to fulfil, this wider mandate. Does it have the mechanisms in place to make sure the oversight of governance can be cascaded through the firm?

Structure of compensation

All the major statements on the reform of compensation in the financial services industry have touched on the concern that compensation has been too short-term and not aligned with the risk profile of the business.

There are, of course, many aspects to this. Regulators have asked questions about whether the overall ratio of variable to fixed pay (known as the leverage ratio) is too high. As a result, a number of firms have rebalanced compensation, increasing base salaries by as much as 100 per cent with an offsetting reduction in bonus pools. As well as reducing leverage, this can improve employee perception of compensation at a time when bonus pools are highly uncertain.

But the main issue raised by regulatory intervention has undoubtedly been the use and design of deferred compensation. As a result almost all firms in the banking sector, and many beyond it, are reviewing their deferral policies.

It is now standard practice for a proportion of bonus to be deferred over three years or more − 60 per cent of bonus or more is typical for the highest earners. Circumstances under which the deferred portion may be forfeited could include a material failure of risk management, personal misconduct, or a severe downturn in financial performance.

Deferral arrangements are generally simple: cash or shares. But there has been much discussion recently about the use of contingent convertibles (cocos) in compensation design. In principle, these have some attractive properties. They are less risky than shares for the participant and so can overcome some of the growing concerns about overexposure through increased levels of share deferral. Yet the bank still gains beneficial capital treatment through using them.

There remains a lack of regulatory clarity about what does and does not count for favourable capital treatment. It may be that the features required (for example, the regulator having an option to convert) may be seen to create too much uncertainty for an employee-compensation instrument. Firms are exploring simpler structures in the absence of regulatory clarity. These include simple cash-deferral arrangements that change nature in the event of a trigger event, such as the core Tier 1 capital ratio falling below a prescribed level. If the trigger is activated, the deferred cash payment may simply be delayed until the capital position of the bank recovers. Alternatively, it may convert to equity. These structures keep many of the elements of simple cash deferral, while retaining an element of protection for the firm if the bank comes under financial duress. We can expect this to be a field of further exploration and innovation in the coming years.

As mentioned earlier, the leverage ratio is moving up the agenda for debate. In Europe, CRD3 requires firms to have a policy on this ratio resulting in a number of firms reducing leverage through rebalancing — that is, increasing fixed pay in exchange for bonus. The European Banking Authority (EBA) has announced that it will review this area in 2012. The implied threat for firms is that if the EBA is not satisfied with what it finds, an onerous binding technical standard could be issued that requires firms to reduce pay leverage drastically. The potential unintended consequences of such a move are clear. Mandating a reduction in leverage is likely to have little impact on pay levels and would simply result in further shifts between bonus and fixed pay. This would increase banks' fixed-cost levels, making them less rather than more resilient to financial shocks. Banks need to get on the front foot to make the case for the current highly variable pay systems in operation, in terms of the cost flexibility and performance focus that they provide.

Incorporating risk into performance measures

Before the financial crisis, risk-adjusted measures were not widely used in remuneration in the sector. PwC's 2009 survey, *Financial services reward: the new paradigm*, showed that only 30 per cent of firms in July 2008 used a risk-adjusted measure, but two-thirds of the remaining firms were evaluating or implementing these measures. The situation is already substantially different. Most firms now use risk-adjusted metrics as part of the bonus-funding process. Where robust risk measures do not exist for particular risk categories, firms are looking to supplement them through a mix of quantitative and qualitative risk commentary.

Banks require a structured, yet discretionary, approach to incorporate risk into the remuneration process. This provides a framework that allows compensation to be viewed through performance, risk and other relevant lenses. All big banks have reviewed their approach to bonus funding in the light of regulatory intervention. In almost all cases the result of this review has been more input from control functions into the bonus process, and in particular a greater role for risk information.

The use of detailed risk-adjusted performance in determining remuneration in the banking industry became widespread during 2010 in response to regulatory pressure. Although the Financial Services Authority (FSA) Remuneration Code and the FSB Implementation Standards both referred to risk-adjustment in 2009, the regulatory focus in 2010 was on remuneration structures and, in particular, deferral. In 2011, the focus of both the FSA and individual firms shifted towards risk-adjustment in determining the performance on which bonuses are based and the role played by the risk function in the remuneration process.

As risk-adjustment has gained prominence as a concept, the role of economic profit in bonus funding has also increased, encouraged by the endorsement of regulators. But only a small minority of banks use economic profit in a formulaic way to determine bonus pool outcomes. Instead, economic profit, including year-on-year developments and performance against plan, has gained prominence as one of the factors in a process for determining bonuses. Others include financial performance information, qualitative and quantitative risk metrics, non-financial factors and assessment of market competitiveness of pay.

The inherent shortcomings in a single metric to determine bonus funding, combined with the extraordinary circumstances of the past two years, have had an impact on the approach of banks in this area. Their focus has been on making sure that senior management and the remuneration committee have a range of metrics and perspectives on risk to help them make an informed judgement about bonus funding — rather than a series of adjustments to economic profit to derive a single performance statistic to drive bonus funding.

Where we are now: the glass half full

Regulators can point to significant changes in remuneration practices across a number of areas. The recent FSB review of compliance with regulation shows that big firms have fully adopted the requirements on governance and design of compensation.

Independent remuneration committees now oversee remuneration policy and the specific remuneration outcomes for staff perceived to be significant risk-takers within banks, representing a broader remit. Risk and control functions have appropriate input into remuneration decisions and into the design of new incentive plans. The remuneration of control functions is determined with appropriate independence from the business areas they oversee.

The requirements on remuneration design have also been widely adopted. For senior risk-takers, the majority of bonus payments are denominated in shares or other instruments deferred for at least three years. These can then be clawed back if significant failings are uncovered over the deferral period.

The consideration of risk in discussions on remuneration outcomes has increased significantly. Not only has the sophistication of the data provided to remuneration committees improved, but the chief risk officer now generally attends the committee meeting where bonuses are determined, so as to be available for questioning by non-executive directors.

Finally, enhanced disclosures mean that external stakeholders, and in particular investors, have a much clearer view of remuneration processes at banks, enabling them to make better decisions about remuneration-related risks.

Where we are now: the glass half empty

How much has really been achieved? Cynics would say that the changes are a triumph of form over substance, that compensation changes are a thin veneer covering the continuation of previous practices. That would be unfair. But it is valid to ask how much the amount of time that has been devoted to regulatory change has contributed to sound and effective risk management.

In this context there are three areas where more could be achieved.

Information overload

The focus on risk-adjustment of performance has led to widespread use of risk-adjusted financial measures, risk dashboards and the like. In many cases these have led to more thoughtful analysis of the information required to show where risks are arising. But there is a risk of remuneration committees losing the important messages among all the information. The answer to sound risk management does not generally lie in inch-thick data packs. Instead, the focus needs to be on asking simple, yet challenging questions of management and the risk function. How has the risk profile changed over the year? Which risks are the hardest to measure? What are the main areas where increased risk could flatter performance? Failures of risk management are often less to do with failure of models and more to do with failure to ask the simple questions.

Behavioural change

While significant amounts of work have been done on risk-adjusting bonus pools and ensuring risk and compliance metrics are factored into individual balanced scorecards, how much of this is filtering down to decision-making at the front line? Are managers using regulation as a catalyst to truly embed the change to a more risk-sensitive mindset, or do they view their role as protecting their staff from more regulatory change? To be effective, remuneration changes need to result in different individual pay outcomes and the prioritisation of different behaviour. Otherwise little will be achieved. Given the stresses currently being suffered by the industry now is perhaps not the time to pass judgement on how much the culture of banking has changed. Unfortunately we will need to wait for the next economic upswing to find out.

Sharing value

Of course the elephant in the room is quantum. Regulators have studiously avoided getting embroiled in debates about the appropriate quantum of pay, but the debates will not go away. Increased capital requirements mean that shareholders need to shoulder a greater burden in the generation of banking profits.

So they should surely enjoy a greater share of the spoils. In 2010 banks continued to invest in compensation on the basis of an expected strong economic rebound. In 2011 the talk was of a reset to compensation. In practice banks are looking hard at how to return to acceptable levels of return on equity, including the role of pay levels. But banks need to get better at telling their investors how they think about sharing value between employees and shareholders, and why their approach is fair and sustainable.

It's not all about the pay

It is important to recognise that the underlying aim of the regulations is to make sure that compensation plays an appropriate role in keeping a firm's entire operations consistent with and supportive of sound risk management.

Changes to compensation are important. But there is a danger in taking an isolated reward design solution that has the appearance of progress but little in the way of underlying change. For the outcome to be successful, compensation changes must be viewed in the context of a firm's wider enterprise risk-management approach. Equally, compensation must be aligned with how the firm is actually run and performance is measured. Alignment is the watchword.

The process should ideally start with a coherent articulation of risk strategy, profile and appetite. This then cascades into the supporting processes, information, infrastructure and reward systems to support strong business performance and capital management. Any future approach to compensation should be integrated within a multidisciplinary approach. As well as addressing the technical aspects of risk management, firms are paying more attention to the question of risk culture — how to define it, measure it and influence it — in which task compensation is just one lever for change.

Delivering and embedding such a model constitutes a major change programme. It often requires commitment to delivering a sustainable change in the culture of the organisation, which is difficult to achieve. This wider requirement should not delay implementation of the specifics. But the importance of a coherent approach — and the limitation of any specific initiatives taken in isolation — should not be underestimated. As ever, no single initiative will provide the answer. Success is driven by a coherent set of mutually reinforcing actions, undertaken within the context of strong leadership and a vision for the organisation.

Financial practitioners know that, especially in banking, compensation is important in its own right. Compensation did not cause the financial boom and bust, but it did add fuel to the fire. From the regulators' point of view, compensation practices are a highly visible indicator of the quality of a firm's governance. Those that get compensation wrong are more likely to get other things wrong as well. We can expect regulators to take a sustained interest in this area for the foreseeable future. So change must be in substance as well as form.

5

A client's view

SIR MARTIN SORRELL

For anyone involved in the financial markets, as a trading institution, an investor or a corporate client, the past three years have been turbulent indeed. We saw the widespread drying up of liquidity then the catastrophic collapse in trust following the bankruptcy of Lehman Brothers in 2008. Now the markets are struggling with Europe's sovereign debt crisis, which continues to burden the financial sector and the real economy.

As a corporate user of the financial markets and wholesale banks, the company I run, WPP, has not been immune from any of these developments. We, like everyone else, suffered from the low to non-existent liquidity in financial markets between 2007 and early 2009. We experienced the force of the subsequent economic slowdown, and are acutely conscious that continuing financial uncertainty and instability threaten to choke off investment in the economy at large and delay, or even in the worst case reverse, economic recovery.

But I have a number of deeper concerns about the present situation as it affects the financial markets and the banking industry — concerns that go beyond the state of the cycle to the fundamentals of managing the global market economy.

I worry that we have not begun to learn the lessons from the current financial crisis — and that until we do we will be poorly positioned to prevent the next one. I worry that too many people — in banks, among investment institutions and in governments — have been behaving as if it is going to be possible to return reasonably rapidly to business as usual in the markets, when history shows that events of this magnitude take several years to work through and resolve themselves. And I worry about leadership in the crisis — or rather the lack of it.

Political leadership is crucial for the return of confidence to the markets: leadership in getting control of fiscal deficits across the industrial world, leadership in creating the right governance framework for the euro, leadership in ensuring the free flow of capital and goods and preventing a slide back into national policymaking and protectionism. And not least, leadership in creating a system of supervision for financial markets that is both globally coherent and finely tuned to excessive and destabilising accumulations of risk.

To put these points another way: we underestimate at our peril the scale of the shock created by the 2008 financial collapse and the gravity and complexity of the failure it laid bare. For the corporate sector, it continues to have deep and enduring consequences — more, probably, than for consumers.

WPP is a fairly typical corporate user of the financial markets. We use investment banks for their expertise in areas where it is uneconomic for us to employ that expertise full-time ourselves, such as for advice on merger and acquisition activity, and as counterparts to financial transactions where necessary. And we use commercial banks for treasury services, trading and hedging.

We use derivative products to hedge financial market risks arising from the company's commercial activities, such as fluctuations in interest rates and exchange rates — risks that, if unhedged, could reduce our income or the value of our assets.

We don't use complex financial products, as often I don't understand them, and like other much more intelligent people such as Warren Buffett, I am suspicious of things I don't understand. But we do use less complex financial products to reduce currency risks and hedge balance-sheet risks such as future acquisition payments.

So what was our experience when the crisis broke in 2008? First, our access to the US commercial paper market for our working capital needs was closed off when that market froze. We were forced to refinance bank debt in the bond markets in 2009, when we would have preferred to wait until markets were calmer.

But at another level, the effect of the Lehman crisis was even more profound. It made us, like other companies, very sensitive and concerned about liquidity risks. In general, corporate clients are worried not just about efficiency and effectiveness, but also about liquidity. This concern is not going to go away any time soon.

That is why it is so damaging to pretend that we can get back to some semblance of the old normality in running the financial system while memories of the Lehman collapse are fresh. This has not happened yet: interbank lending still takes place but on a very short-term basis, and nobody knows when or if that will change. Sovereign borrowers, those former havens of safety, are now being battered by markets as much as the banks. These are all aftershocks from the events of autumn 2008, and in particular of what I call the 'too-big-to-fail weekend' when the US government allowed Lehman Brothers to go down. They mean that for the foreseeable future I don't think there will be a return to 'normality' for anyone involved with the financial markets.

As the crisis drags on, it increasingly appears that the steps governments and others have taken to address it have been inadequate. The response of European and other authorities around the world has been less than reassuring: it has simply been poor.

In my view the crisis reflects not so much insufficient regulation as a catastrophic failure of supervision at multiple levels. Clearly, as has often been the case with financial bubbles from the Dutch tulip mania onwards, there is a collective responsibility. We all got carried away in the boom, and it behoves us all to learn from that. We all know about the competitive pressures fostered by short-term goals for shareholder value and returns, and the culture of excessive risk-taking that resulted. But it was the failure to supervise − by bank regulators, bank boards and bank shareholders − that turned the boom into such a disorderly bust.

That failure reflects a deeper myopia. Put simply, the authorities and society at large did not fully understand the consequences of the repeal of the Glass-Steagall Act in the US and of the Big Bang changes to financial markets in the UK. They failed to give sufficient consideration to the dangers in combining financial market trading activity with commercial and retail banking under one roof. As is now painfully apparent, these are fundamentally different activities requiring different management skills. And they demanded a fundamentally different approach to official supervision of financial institutions.

Supervisors need to have a much broader ability to conduct prudential checks on individual banking groups. Central banks should have a much clearer view of the big picture − of institutions' total exposure to sectors and markets on both the asset and liability sides − and therefore be in a better position to provide guidance when an individual bank has potentially troublesome outsized exposure.

Such a singular focus on supervision would have highlighted much sooner the dangerous exposure of banks to hedge funds or to the off-balance-sheet vehicles that constituted the

'shadow banking system', for example, or the risky concentrations of US housing-related assets — and potentially permitted
the authorities to take avoiding action. Had EU supervisors and
governments been honest about concentrations and valuations
of sovereign assets on the books of European banks, rather
than conducting a series of meaningless 'stress tests' in
2009 – 11 that ignored these risks, some of the extreme turbu-
lence of the past year on European and global markets might
have been avoided.

It is probably true to say that it is not possible to turn the
clock back to Glass-Steagall or to put the genie of 'universal
banking' back in its bottle. But in the US and Europe there is
now a common desire to limit the resulting risks. The problem
is that different countries are trying to do this in different
ways: in the US through the tortuous efforts to impose the
Volcker Rule that seeks to ban banks from proprietary trading
and to limit their ownership of hedge funds; in the UK by ring-
fencing a bank's retail activities from investment banking as
proposed by the Vickers Commission. These initiatives may
well satisfy national political imperatives. But they also create
international confusion, and if implemented in isolation will
simply not work or make the overall system safer. There will be
differences in detail — concerning what rule applies to whom,
and how — and of jurisdiction and extra-territoriality, all of
which will create cost as well as opportunities for gaming the
system.

In a world of large, diversified, global financial institutions,
no country can regulate or supervise in isolation; international
cooperation is mandatory. I would say that despite the ambi-
tious promises made by the Group of 20 leaders in the heat of
the crisis in 2008, we have seen the semblance of international
cooperation more than the reality.

The US has been ploughing its own furrow determined by
political mood and electoral calendar. European Union leaders

have been perennially on the back foot, caught between the conflicting desires to shore up the euro, restore financial discipline and protect their domestic banks. Other territories — in Asia, for example — have not joined in the current regulatory drive with anything like the same zeal, creating the risk of regulatory arbitrage, a phenomenon that has never fostered financial stability.

It is not therefore surprising that markets are unsettled. What governments should do to regenerate confidence in the system is give more autonomy to supra-national institutions such as the IMF and the Financial Stability Board, combined with a stronger brief to coordinate monetary stability with national central banks. Politicians, with their shorter time horizons, are ill-equipped to provide the deep systemic reform required.

In the absence of such cooperation, we need to be clear that the problem of some banks being 'too big to fail' is still with us. In a global marketplace, it is impossible to let major international banks fail without putting the very functionality of financial markets at risk. Nor does it seem feasible to cap the business activities or institutional size of international banking groups by law, nor is it realistic to expect that other participants could easily replace them. It is almost impossible to isolate a problem in post-Lehman financial markets: if one large player (or debtor) fails, markets will quickly shy away from the next possible domino, promising an even bigger mess.

Meanwhile, the various national and regional regulatory machines are in overdrive and will probably generate a surfeit of rules that will create more problems for the functioning of free markets and the real economy than they resolve. There is a lot of pressure, for example, to tighten regulation of the use and trading of derivatives. Such actions would be distinctly unwelcome if they impaired companies' ability to hedge their risks.

They would also be highly ironic. It was not, after all, the non-financial corporations that drove the successive waves of the financial crisis. It will therefore be hardly fair if they have to suffer from regulatory efforts that increase bureaucracy and cost.

6

Megatrends shaping the corporate banking landscape – a European outlook

HANS-PAUL BÜRKNER

In the wake of considerable market turmoil in recent years, corporate banking executives in Europe are being compelled to fundamentally strengthen their businesses to prepare for a range of possible scenarios. These include stuttering but positive growth, a Japan-style 'lost decade', even a renewed full-blown crisis. As economic doubts linger, underscored by more imminent concerns over sovereign debt, the only certainty seems to be a volatile and intense competitive climate.

Yet beyond the pressures of day-to-day operations, corporate banks in Europe must also react to broader, underlying trends that will affect how their clients — and in turn how they themselves — do business. The most powerful of these forces, the 'megatrends', are the continuing process of globalisation; the shifting structures of the new economy; advancing technology; and the 'new normal' financial environment. Institutions must also put the lessons of the past five years to good use in navigating their way forward.

Ultimately, European corporate banks must react and adapt to the megatrends — as well as learn from the past — if they hope to build a strong and resilient foundation for the challenges yet to come.

Globalisation 2.0

Some pundits claim that the financial crisis of 2008 – 09 and its aftermath will curtail globalisation. And they raise some legitimate points. For example, euro-zone economic fears have indeed reinforced protectionist views to some degree. Regulators are demanding that multinational banks match their local assets and liabilities more closely. Disruptions such as those caused by the 2011 earthquake in Japan may convince some companies to shorten or domesticate their supply chains.

Yet despite these realities, the sweeping trend towards interconnectedness — which could be termed 'Globalisation 2.0' — will continue to gain momentum. Indeed, this trend has already gone far beyond the early 'Globalisation 1.0' days characterised by mature economies importing goods from developing ones and by early outsourcing initiatives. Simply put, corporate banking clients of virtually all shapes and sizes will continue to expand internationally, and leading banks will have a powerful incentive to follow them. For example, the Boston Consulting Group (BCG) forecasts that the share of global GDP generated in the Asia-Pacific region will rise to almost 40 per cent by 2020, compared with around 30 per cent in 2010. Roughly as much foreign direct investment is now flowing from emerging markets to mature ones as in the other direction — upending a multi-year trend. The number of companies from Brazil, Russia, India and China (the BRIC countries) in the *Fortune* Global 500 has more than tripled, from 27 companies in 2005 to 83 in 2011. In terms of market capitalisation, four of the top ten banks in the world are now based in China.[1]

Megatrends shaping the corporate banking landscape

The effects of Globalisation 2.0 on corporate banks in Europe will be significant. On the client side, more companies, even fairly small ones, will be active across borders. Growing enterprises such as those based in the BRIC countries will need a full range of banking services as they sell automobiles, computers and myriad other goods to the rest of the world. The potential revenues to be gained from these trends will be sizeable, but capturing them will require a nimble and creative approach. Indeed, exactly what kind of innovative financial-supply-chain services will be needed? How might the sales forces of domestic European banks capture the business of BRIC multinationals expanding abroad?

Globalisation 2.0 will also affect the competitive landscape in Europe. New rivals may potentially emerge from the BRIC countries to replicate in corporate banking what some aggressive companies from rapidly developing economies (RDEs) have achieved in other industries. And as BRIC banks follow their clients into established markets, competition with both local and global-titan banks will unquestionably heat up.

On the operational side, European corporate banks will face increasing choices about how to internationalise their back offices, which they must do in order to capture scale and seamlessly serve multinational clients. One option is to create 'international product factories' capable of serving clients in different markets. Corporate banks can also emulate many retail banks by pursuing more offshoring and outsourcing solutions (although political and regulatory considerations in some markets may block this path to a degree).

Ultimately, no large corporate bank in Europe or elsewhere will be immune to the effects of Globalisation 2.0. Moreover, growth-oriented banks will be tempted by the RDEs. BCG estimates that over 40 per cent of total global revenue growth in corporate banking between 2009 and 2019 will come from the BRIC nations.

One notable caveat is that banks must obviously tread carefully in the globalisation arena. Corporate banking is in many ways a local business with significant barriers to entry, especially in the small- and mid-cap segments. There are numerous examples of banks whose forays into international markets have ended in costly failure. Such episodes, in addition to regulatory pressure and capital scarcity, may result in fewer banks embarking on foreign growth sprees.

The new economy

The coming years will be highly challenging for companies in virtually all industry sectors — as well as for the banks that serve them. Five key trends will exert the greatest impact.

Increasing competitive intensity

In September 2011, the IMF predicted euro-zone economic growth of just 1.6 per cent in 2011 and 1.1 per cent in 2012, a downgrade prompted by fears over Europe's debt crisis, with growth in the United States expected to be 1.5 per cent in 2011 and 1.8 per cent in 2012. With the likelihood of such modest economic expansion, the race for clients, market share and profits will be more frenzied than ever. The chief implication for corporate banks in Europe is that clients will be increasingly sensitive about margins and fees. Weaker competitors will start to compete on prices, and clients will pressure incumbent banks to lower theirs, forcing incumbents to become more efficient. Also, product competition will potentially heat up as some institutions develop specialised offerings such as asset-based lending.

Industry-specific banking needs

Some industries are sweet spots for corporate banks because of their rapid growth rates and specific product needs. Such dynamics are linked to the long-term shift from manufacturing to services in the global economy, and thus from credit-heavy banking relationships to a greater mix of transactions and deposits. In Europe, for example, corporate banks often find that clients focused on services or on wholesale/retail trade can have 1.5 – 2 times the revenue potential in transaction banking and other fee-based products of clients that are focused on manufacturing.

Continuing consolidation

Globalisation and increasing competitive intensity will continue to spur consolidation in many industries. European corporate banks that want to serve leading companies as well as up-and-coming mid-market ones will need top investment banking capabilities. Furthermore, cross-border consolidation should increase the number of clients that look to their banks for multi-country solutions across payments and trade finance.

Closer supply-chain integration

The trend we have seen in recent years towards deeper integration along supply chains will continue, although it will undoubtedly be affected by other global trends, such as rising energy costs (which will increase transport costs). As companies integrate with their business partners more closely (both domestically and across borders), they will be looking for parallel financial supply-chain services from their banks.

The search for top talent

BCG's casework with corporate banking clients in Europe and around the world has consistently identified talent management as a growing area of concern. Competition for top talent – such as senior relationship managers (RMs), bad-loan workout specialists and investment bankers who are experienced in priority emerging markets – is hotter than ever.

Banks will also need managers with skills in such areas as leveraging new IT capabilities and optimising end-to-end loan processes. As the baby-boom generation begins to retire, finding the talent needed to navigate a large corporate bank through the evolving megatrends will be more challenging than ever. Corporate banks must meet this challenge by forging a clear strategy for talent acquisition, management and retention. This initiative is especially critical in Europe, where demographic trends are unfavourable and labour markets have to fight against the attractions of major hubs such as London and the fast-growing BRICs.

Advancing technology

Despite continuing advances in technology, few corporate banks in Europe or elsewhere have the platforms in place to ensure leading functionality and connectivity for clients, as well as efficient and effective sales-to-service processes. Similarly, few institutions possess risk, liquidity and capital-management systems capable of delivering the full depth of information needed in today's corporate banking environment. These shortcomings result from a variety of factors, including investment limits and the often low priority of the corporate banking unit compared with the bank's (usually larger) retail business unit.

Indeed, while many retail institutions have powerful customer-information platforms, numerous corporate banks still have disjointed management-information systems in which applications for core businesses such as cash management and trade finance, for example, exist on different platforms — and contain different client information that is difficult to compare. At some corporate banks in Europe, extensive manual processes are still required, complex legacy sales tools hinder sales force productivity and lending processes remain paper-intensive.

Yet in our age of ubiquitous connectivity, expanding bandwidth, massive computing power and pervasive wireless connectivity, corporate banking clients continue to invest in better financial systems. Organisations of every size are trying to connect more seamlessly with their banks – either through sophisticated online data-transfer functions for small and mid-size clients or through deeper integration with large, corporate, enterprise resource planning systems. This growing need will have important implications for corporate banks in Europe and elsewhere that are trying to increase their share in transaction banking. Clients, of course, are looking for a variety of benefits: better ease of use (to reduce the amount of internal training they need to provide); greater breadth in the products and services they can access through self-service portals; better integration and customisation; and improved two-way communication.

Moreover, banks that can build deep, rich, real-time data and analytics capabilities will be able to develop a holistic view of each client relationship – including product-utilisation patterns as well as risk, liquidity and capital factors. Such banks will be able to significantly improve product targeting, pricing and risk management.

Ultimately, corporate banks need to build platforms that automate core processes involving account opening, lending and transaction banking on an end-to-end basis – from the customer to the back office. Automation and algorithms that catch and correct data-entry errors will result in higher rates of straight-through processing, greater client satisfaction and lower costs. In areas where human processing is still required, advances in data storage and imaging technology will allow greater use of centralised, offshore processing centres. In addition, advances in automated decision intelligence will allow more sophisticated treatment of loan applications and fraud detection, as well as improved client monitoring.

Banks will, of course, need to remember that reliance on models and automated tools can be dangerous if this dependence attempts to replace human judgement in critical areas. But advanced intelligence engines hold promise both as cost savers in simple decisions such as micro- and small-business loans and as electronic aids to prioritisation that can help staff focus on the right client files and risk decisions.

The new normal financial environment

Before the financial crisis of 2008 – 09, corporate banking executives could focus largely on client acquisition and revenue growth. Today, they need to look in another direction as well, towards balance sheets and financial markets. They must pay far more attention to capital usage, risk management and liquidity than they have in the past. Indeed, before the crisis, the truly discriminating factor for investments was return on equity or RoE (ie, RoE greater than 15 per cent or so). Now it is capital and funding. In essence, banks have moved from a profit-and-loss perspective to a balance-sheet perspective.

This new outlook is also being driven by regulatory changes such as Basel III that raise the cost of capital and increase term funding. Basel III is certainly hitting financial institutions from many different directions. Key parts of the corporate banking business will be required to hold more capital as a buffer against potential losses — capital that is both scarcer and more expensive. Moreover, Basel III rules on both liquidity and corporate deposits will require painful adjustments, as will changes that add steps, complexity and therefore costs to core processes such as commercial lending. Some countries, such as Switzerland, are adding additional layers of regulation on top of Basel III. Overall, Basel III will have a fundamental impact on the strategic choices of both banks and their clients. One example is that high-quality corporate banking clients in

Europe may move increasingly towards issuing debt instead of borrowing. For banks, such a development could make the lending business unprofitable in some markets, at least if costs cannot be passed on to clients.

Moreover, after the bubble years of driving for revenue and market-share growth, the financial crisis reminded the corporate banking industry that risk management is a major differentiator between competitors. Some banks have succeeded in building sustainably profitable corporate banking franchises while others have been seen apparent success disappear under the impact of severe losses. Building superior risk-management capabilities in corporate banking is never easy; it requires senior executive vision and sustained leadership across multiple dimensions to create a culture of risk awareness and accountability at every level. Such a culture includes the knowledge at loan origination that capital and funding are scarce and expensive — knowledge that needs to be supported by a robust funds transfer-pricing system that enables transparency.

The first line of defence is the front office — as opposed to the front office pressing the accelerator when the risk department tries to step on the brakes. Overall, to build a strong risk culture, there are five basic steps that corporate banks can take:

1. *Maintain the strong independence of risk-control functions.* The risk function needs to get out of its ghetto. What is needed is a culture of true risk management — not just risk reporting and upward delegation. Risk managers must be properly compensated and recognised, and their independence from the front office guaranteed. They must also be encouraged to be proactive. 'Risk functions need to go looking for trouble rather than waiting for trouble to find them' is how one risk specialist has described it.

2. *Ensure senior-management competence in risk management.* Those banks that have best weathered the past five years typically possess a wealth of accumulated experience in risk management across sales, product development and general management functions. They also tend to set aside time for thoughtful consideration of risk trends and scenarios, with a premium placed on business judgement rather than having the risk analysts slice and dice the risk data into lengthy and complex reports that go unread.

3. *Adopt incentives that take risk-management performance into account.* The principal issue is not bonus levels alone but the need to explicitly link bonuses to risk-adjusted performance over a sufficient period of time. Some banks have rewarded RMs purely on the basis of loan volumes and revenues rather than long-term economic profit.

4. *Encourage healthy debate.* Deals, especially the most complex ones, must be discussed in depth. Even deals with prestige clients brought in by top-performing RMs must be openly scrutinised. The role of risk committees in fostering such discussions is essential, as is the role of senior risk specialists. The latter are critical to productive thought partnering with sales and other executives. Banks whose risk analysts are junior staff limited to generating reports are missing a significant opportunity.

5. *Improve risk data and analytics.* Banks must invest to improve their data gathering, reporting and analytics on their clients. Outside observers are often startled to learn that some well-known corporate banks struggle to compile holistic risk data on major clients, to match risk-department data with finance-department data on loans and to quickly identify deteriorating loans for handling by their special loans groups.

Ultimately, corporate banks in Europe must pursue

numerous initiatives — in addition to improving risk management — in the new normal financial environment. These initiatives include the following:

- Strive to acquire quality clients and develop a distribution model that effectively serves each client segment.
- Form a clear view of segment and market priorities.
- Drive pricing that is risk-based and adjusted for real funding costs.
- Devise an efficient target operating model and manage costs aggressively.
- Embed principles of liquidity management and capital lightness into strategic planning.
- Develop a culture of end-to-end transparency that includes tracking and reporting on a segment-specific basis across revenues, costs, loan volumes and economic capital — as well as across client, product and sales-force data.
- Create a high-performance organisation based on leadership, collaboration, accountability and performance management.
- Focus on clients' overall profitability across products (both assets and liabilities); build technical platforms for measuring this profitability and for offering settlement (central clearing) and cash services; strive to develop excellence in multiple products — not just lending.

Only by achieving many of these goals can corporate banks optimally position themselves for the challenges yet to come.

Learning from the past

After reviewing the experiences of top performers in recent years and speaking to senior corporate banking executives, BCG has identified a set of lessons that no corporate banking CEO in Europe (or elsewhere) should forget.

The first lesson is *always keep the balance sheet at the top of the agenda*. Corporate banks should fully factor risk, as well as liquidity and capital management, into their long-term strategies, operational planning, and day-to-day management. This fundamental rule was overlooked by many of the lowest-performing corporate banks in recent years, as too many focused on revenue and market share — not factoring in the 'real' costs of risk, liquidity, and capital — when making lending and pricing decisions.

The second lesson is that *corporate banks should manage their businesses like a portfolio*, with an 'over the cycle' point of view. Businesses such as commercial real estate and equipment finance can be profitable, but banks must be disciplined enough to monitor the growth of such businesses, especially during 'good' years. It is also critical not to let one or two sectors that appear to be highly lucrative grow too large in the portfolio. A collapse in these areas can create painful loan losses as well as eliminate a significant portion of the bank's overall revenue stream.

International or 'out of footprint' expansion provides another lesson: *corporate banks must be extra cautious outside their home markets*. It has always been extremely difficult to transfer a successful business model in one country into a new environment. Credit-led expansion, in particular, can be dangerous, especially if competitors have either superior knowledge of client risks or better capabilities in valuing and managing collateral. It is all too easy for a new entrant to end up with customers that have been rejected by entrenched local banks which have superior market knowledge and a less urgent need to quickly acquire clients to cover the costs of a newly expanded sales force. This is a lesson that banks must keep in mind as they consider how to take advantage of the rapid growth in corporate banking in rapidly developing economies.

Lastly, and most importantly in the long run, *corporate banks must cultivate deep client relationships.* A salient point, one that some institutions learned the hard way during the 2008 – 09 crisis, is that having a quality client portfolio is the most critical driver of performance as well as the most fundamental element of any risk-management strategy. Leading banks are systematically developing deep, long-term relationships with first-rate clients – companies that possess robust businesses, strong management teams and broad banking needs. Unfortunately, during the financial crisis, many fast-growing banks discovered that their rapid revenue expansion was really just a form of adverse selection. Too many of their loans could not be repaid, and their low-quality clients either were acquired or faced bankruptcy.

*

Finally, taking the long view, it is clear that major financial upheavals such as the one we have witnessed over the past five years – dire as they may seem for a time – present opportunities, not just threats, to institutions that develop the most robust business models and the most creative strategies. Leading corporate banks use highly uncertain times to their advantage, gaining market share and a competitive edge over slower-moving rivals that simply try to endure crises and hope for the best. The leaders seize the moment to begin the process of becoming a truly blue-chip player. In the end, corporate banks can largely control their own destinies by determining which type of institution they aspire to be.

7

In defence of the indefensible: financial innovation and complex financial instruments

AVINASH D. PERSAUD

Introduction

The explosive increase in derivative instruments over the past two decades — they now exceed the size of their underlying cash markets many times over — runs against the better instincts of many outside the financial sector. To them, it seems unsavoury for the tail to wag the dog. A popular view of the financial crisis is that it was caused by bankers, pulling out of their back pockets newly invented instruments of mass destruction, throwing them into a crowd of bewildered consumers, grabbing the money and running away. More prosaically, others argue that the central business model of banks is to take advantage of asymmetric information: to overcharge their clients for instruments that are more complex and opaque than they need or can understand. As evidence, investors

99

nursing heavy losses following the meltdown of the credit markets in 2008 – 09 show off fat prospectuses of credit derivative instruments they purchased, filled with pages of impenetrable legalese, even before you get to the small print. They ask how they could ever have been expected to understand it all. In these popular narratives, financial innovation is merely a route to egregious profit.

As a young analyst in the late 1980s, I recall Paul Thrush, then treasurer in London of UBS, a global financial services company, admonishing his traders if they expressed surprise at an adverse payout of an instrument they held in their books. He would remind them that they should never hold an instrument they did not fully understand. It is certainly worth asking why we should be expected to pay asset managers who lose our savings by buying things they do not understand. But in the current crisis popular anger is with the egregiously well-paid bankers and not with their slightly less well-paid clients. And banks understand their political vulnerabilities during a crisis when they are dependent on government support. They eschew lengthy high-profile trials that would pore over every detail of their behaviour and opt for paying out large settlements while not accepting blame — which still leaves a strong whiff of guilt.

Politicians respond

Banning instruments

Faced with a crisis in which billions of dollars of taxpayers' money have been channelled into saving the financial system, politicians are commanded by newspapers and public opinion to deliver urgent, decisive and bold action, to seize the culprits and pursue retribution — all so that the crisis could never be repeated, of course. At the highest level, crashes are simply caused by the preceding boom. But the detail of financial crises is complex. They have many proximate causes and interrelationships. The line between victim and perpetrator is often blurred. There are seldom any genuine quick fixes.

However, regulatory caution is interpreted as reluctance to act and this angers the electorate. Occasionally, there is so much anger that it provides sufficient cover for the underemployed to camp out in city centres or to stage some other kind of disruption to embarrass and annoy the government of the day. Outlawing instruments that many finger as dangerous, with a swashbuckling wave of the legislative axe, fits the political requirement perfectly.

The German ban on 'short-selling' (selling an instrument ahead of buying it) is a good example of this response. Anger about short-selling was fuelled by tales of cold-blooded foreign speculators selling short the stocks of innocent local businesses, so as to push financial market ratios to a point where bank covenants would be invoked unless the company issued more stock, or performed some similar self-fulfilling contortion. This would then validate the initial decline in the stock price, allowing the short-seller to reap excessive rewards (by selling high and buying low).

Forcing all instruments on to exchanges

In similar vein, politicians are easily seduced by the idea that the reason all instruments do not trade on exchanges is solely the traders' desire to avoid transparency and reporting. This is an extension of the idea articulated above that banks are trying to preserve an abuse of asymmetrical information. Stories abound of shady activities taking place in 'dark pools'. This leads politicians to call for everything to be brought into the bright light of exchanges. If traders do not wish to trade complex instruments on exchanges, where pricing, quantities and terms are available for all to scrutinise, these instruments should not be traded at all, some say.

A financial market 'FDA'

Another common policy response to the notion that it was financial innovation and complexity — so well embodied in 'CDOs-squared' — that tripped up global finance last time around, is the idea that the finance sector should have the equivalent of a Food and Drug Administration (FDA), which would rigorously test new innovations, perhaps for years. Approved instruments would then be sold alongside appropriate health warnings. The newly minted US Consumer Financial Protection Bureau is based on this idea.

These policy responses are flawed for a number of practical reasons and some quite fundamental ones. I shall examine the fundamental flaws, turning first to the notion that all things should be traded on exchanges.

Why forcing all instruments onto an exchange is a bad idea

The revealed preference for different types of trading is not driven by the fault lines of asymmetric information, but by the interests of both sides of a market. Exchanges work best for instruments where the size of the trade is small relative to the market, so the announcement of a bid does not push the price higher, and the announcement of an offer does not push the price lower. This captures well, for the most part, the market for the ordinary shares of large publicly listed companies and it is why the main venue for trading equities is public exchanges.

However, in markets where the instrument being traded is large relative to the market, and the announcement of a bid or offer would move the market away from the bidder or 'offerer', trades are negotiated 'over-the-counter'. If there were an exchange for residential houses that cleared every day, there would be enormous swings in the price of houses depending on the daily match of supply and liquidity for houses of certain sizes, styles, condition, neighbourhood and so forth. It is right that the residential house market has developed as an over-the-counter market and not an exchange-traded one.

Bond and currency markets are usually over-the-counter because, contrary to popular understanding, they are large when taken as a whole, but small with regard to specific instruments. A company might issue one type of share, but it might have several different bond issues outstanding, each with different maturities, coupons and tax treatment, so while the total bonds outstanding may be large, the market for each instrument may be small relative to the size of the instrument. In the case of government bonds, for instance, the majority of trades take place on a few benchmark issues, such as two-year, five-year and ten-year maturities. But the majority of issues outstanding were once benchmark issues and are no longer: for example, last year's ten-year bond has become a nine-year bond. The market for these 'off-the-run' instruments is far less liquid and is a negotiated, not an exchange-traded market.

The currency markets are massive, with turnover exceeding $5 trillion a day; however, the majority of currency transactions are for a forward, futures or swap contract where foreign exchange is delivered on a specific date, and these are negotiated over-the-counter. For example, if you want to exchange Argentinian pesos for Brazilian reals at close of business next Thursday afternoon, this is best negotiated and not announced, lest others become aware of your need for Brazilian reals at the moment you are seeking to deal and squeeze the supply against you beforehand.

Within the same market, exchanges can be used for small trades that will have no price impact; large trades that will have a price impact are traded off-exchange or over-the-counter and then reported through the exchange as a negotiated trade, which is then cleared and settled as an exchange trade.

The negotiated market can be as large as the exchange-traded market. There have been many attempts to put bond and currency markets on an exchange but none have succeeded. What have emerged are electronic venues where market-makers quote indicative prices for small trades as a signal that they are open to offers and bids.

Similarly, it would be pointless to trade derivative instruments, designed for the specific currency needs and risk-tolerances of an exporter, on an exchange — and maybe worse than pointless. Forcing all instruments onto exchanges will lead to increased volatility and create gaps in the market. If all trading takes place on exchanges, it will appear impossible to match specific bids and offers and this will cause liquidity to dry up.

The call for all instruments to be exchange traded is a solution in search of a problem, of which there are many. If post-trade reporting is what the authorities want to see, and they should, this can be made mandatory on or off exchanges. Under the 2004 EU Markets in Financial Instruments Directive (MiFID), market-making firms are already required to report off-exchange trading in instruments that are also traded on regulated exchanges in the European Union. It would not be a great change to require post-trade reporting of all trades wherever they are conducted. Failure to report could lead to large penalties, including the future unenforceability of the contract.

Similarly, if centralised clearing and settlement is what is required to reduce the systemic risks caused by a settlement problem in a derivative market bigger than the underlying cash market, instruments that do not feature centralised clearing and settlement should be discouraged by requiring their holders to put aside some additional capital. There is an argument, from the perspective of systemic stability, for a single regulated company that clears and settles all security transactions. But clearing requires substantial investment in technology innovation, and the experience of equity trading platforms is that the biggest technological strides were spurred on by competition from new players. The authorities can boost both competition and financial stability by ensuring the 'inter-operability' of clearing houses — counterparties choose where they clear their transactions independently of where they trade them and clearers grant fair access to third-party trading venues. This would deliver more financial stability by maximis-ing the opportunity for netting — offsetting positive and nega-tive values — across a wide range of related instruments irrespective of where the best place to trade those instruments is at any one time. Stability can be enhanced by this sort of horizontal integration as opposed to vertical integration of markets. Forcing trading venues and clearers to fight separately for business will also deliver better services and lower costs to users.

Why a financial market FDA will not work

There are two problems with the idea of an FDA for finance — a supervisor of financial innovation, so to speak. First, almost all complex financial instruments are built using a com-bination of simple, seemingly safe, financial instruments. I have not come across yet an 'exotic' option that cannot be derived by a series of puts and calls. As the effects of the 'sum' are greater than the sum of all the parts, these exotic options are invariably cheaper than trying to recreate them by buying the underlying puts and calls separately. Complexity and sim-plicity are not so easy to distinguish.

Second, financial crises are not caused by people doing things they know are risky; they are caused by people doing things they think are safe, and as a result they double up. Bankers did not throw instruments of mass destruction into a crowd of bewildered customers and then run away. Invariably they tried to stuff as many of these instruments into their own back pockets as possible. The real problem of the so-called 'originate and redistribute' model is that those at the centre of it did not redistribute to others but tried to hold on to as much of the originated instruments as possible, thinking they had found a form of alchemy in their computer models where there was return without risk. Banks created all manner of off-balance-sheet, special-purpose vehicles to enable them to hold more of these instruments themselves and leverage themselves to a greater degree than their balance sheet would otherwise allow.

Anointing instruments 'safe' or 'bad' is not going to solve this problem — indeed, it could make matters worse. Instruments are not born with original sin; they become dangerous through excessive, concentrated or distorted uses. This is more likely to happen if some agency has previously announced that such instruments are safe. The very act of so judging them would create moral hazard.

A fundamental defence of complexity

There is a commonly held belief that complex products are not needed, are socially useless and are only there to obfuscate and earn egregious fees for bankers. There is no denying that some of this happens, but the anti-complexity argument is dangerously overdone. Good risk management is not about not taking risks, as risks are all around us; it is about matching liabilities to assets. An insurer that may need to come up with a lot of cash unexpectedly cannot invest the bulk of its portfolio in illiquid assets. It makes no sense for a young pension fund that will have to make a series of cash payments in 20 years' time to own instruments that are expensive (that is, provide a low return) because they offer overnight liquidity. To do so would increase the risk of needing additional payments into the fund to enable it to afford future payouts. Similarly, if a firm's liabilities are complex, forcing it to use only simple instruments will mean that it will have unmatched risks. That is to say, its overall risk exposure will be greater than would be the case if it used a complex instrument to match its complex liabilities more fully. Eschewing complex assets in a complex world creates risk.

Conclusion

Individuals and assets are becoming more footloose and harder to tax. Fiscally constrained states are paring their social commitments and increasingly trying to remove themselves as insurer of last resort. This shifts liabilities back to individuals, who now have to manage the complex interplay of education and health costs, unemployment insurance and retirement, and so on. Managing complex liabilities requires complex assets. To deny asset managers complexity will be to allow risks to be unmatched. Complexity and the innovation required in developing complex instruments is not a scourge, but a necessity.

Nevertheless, people fear complexity. The aim of this chapter has been to challenge common prejudices regarding complexity, but there is no denying that there are genuine issues. Where there are asymmetries of information, complexity can lead to abuse. Complex instruments can be used to destabilise markets. Through complex instruments, market participants can in effect transform themselves into undercapitalised insurers or banks. Complex instruments can mean that the authorities do not know the size and location of macro risks. These are important issues, but they can be addressed without banning innovation and complexity.

The degree of asymmetry in finance can be overstated. A

hundred years ago this asymmetry was captured by the question posed to American financier and banker John Pierpont Morgan: 'Where are the clients' yachts?' Today investment managers at hedge funds have bigger yachts than their bankers. In my experience when at J.P. Morgan in the 1990s, accompanying those selling exotic options to corporate treasurers, it was the corporate treasurers who demanded an extra bit of complexity to reduce the upfront premium they would otherwise have to pay for the instrument. But asymmetries do exist. They are primarily between the 'wholesale' and 'retail' markets, where retail refers to the end-users such as individuals and companies. Instruments sold to retail investors should pass tests regarding their opacity and the ease with which they can be understood. Complex instruments should not be sold directly to retail investors but instead to the professional institutions that help them manage their risks.

If wholesale investors use complex instruments to create false markets through short-selling, this is not just unethical, it is illegal. The authorities must be more forceful in locking up the perpetrators. Banning certain behaviour is better than banning instruments. The definitions of insurance and banking and the associated regulations need to be divorced from institutions and attached to behaviour, so that if a firm uses complex financial instruments to turn itself from an investor into an insurer, it should be regulated as an insurer, with the requisite capital put aside. Where derivative markets are larger than cash markets, the use of central clearing and settlement by market participants should be encouraged; where instruments are deemed too complex for central clearing and settlement, their use can be discouraged through the requirement to set aside additional capital.

One way to limit excessive complexity would be to introduce a small transactions tax. The lesson of the last ten years is that low transaction costs are better than high ones, but near-zero transaction costs may not be good as they allow huge edifices of circular transactions to take place, many times the value of the underlying transaction. These will always be hard to unwind in an orderly fashion. A small transaction tax, which focuses minds on the underlying value of each transaction, would limit socially useless transactions and would be a small price to pay if it preserved needed innovation and complexity.

8

Reputation in financial markets

ALAN MORRISON, WILLIAM WILHELM, RUPERT YOUNGER

Introduction

Historically, bankers prided themselves upon their close client relationships. Many financial transactions were dependent upon trust, and financial professionals stressed the importance of word-of-mouth commitment to the smooth operation of financial markets. The second of the 14 business principles that John Whitehead identified as critical to the prosecution of business at Goldman Sachs stated: 'Our assets are our people, capital, and reputation. If any of these is ever diminished, the last is the most difficult to restore.'[1] For most of the past two centuries, a good reputation was a critical asset in finance.

And yet, notwithstanding the above remarks, recent comments by business leaders and financiers suggest that reputational incentives have changed in recent years. For example, Alan Greenspan, a former chairman of the Federal Reserve System, stated in a 2008 speech: 'In a market system, based on trust, reputation has a significant economic value. I am therefore distressed at how far we have let concerns for reputation slip in recent years.'[2] Steven M. Davidoff, an Ohio State University law professor, remarked in a 2011 *New York Times* blog that 'Reputation is dead on Wall Street ... That is not to say that financiers and financial firms still do not commit foolish misdeeds. Rather, so long as the authorities do not find law-breaking, the penalties are few.'[3]

These opinions are widely held. Many commentators have suggested that reputational incentives have been weakened in recent years and, in line with Davidoff, many have argued that the only real sanctions are legal and regulatory, rather than reputational.[4] Many have gone further, arguing that a breakdown of traditional norms of behaviour, and a concomitant diminution of long-term reputational concerns in financial markets, was the root cause of the recent financial crisis.[5]

Could a return from the large complex bank of today to the prelapsarian world of the investment banking partnership restore morality to financial markets, and hence prevent the recurrence of financial market turmoil? While this is a tempting conclusion, we argue in this chapter that it could not. Changes to market practices, and to the governance arrangements that support them, reflect deeper technological changes. The technological changes, and their real economy consequences, have been playing out for several decades, and they are irreversible. Moreover, and notwithstanding their undesirable side effects, it is not clear *a priori* that the net effect of these changes is negative.

In this chapter, we attempt to understand the changing role of reputation in financial markets. We discuss the relevance of reputation in complex trade, and show how recent changes to the financial and technological environment have altered the role and relevance of reputation. We identify businesses in which reputation is still of critical importance and ones in which it is not. This analysis allows us to identify new conflicts and complexities in the governance of banking firms, and hence to discuss some of the trade-offs that face legislators and bankers as they respond to the trends that we identify. We conclude with some preliminary thoughts regarding the appropriate resolution of these conflicts.

The economic role of reputation in financial markets

Many discussions of reputation are conducted at cross-purposes. Some argue that a firm has reputation by virtue of its visibility; others argue that reputation accrues to institutions or people when their actions accord with a subjective notion of 'virtue', so that, for example, a firm that invests in social programmes is reputable, while one that does not is not. Others equate reputation with an ill-defined notion of 'trust', which is apparently again related to virtue.[6]

In this chapter, we adopt a more precise formulation of reputation. For us, reputation is relevant when important aspects of a transaction cannot easily be measured or recorded. For example, it is hard for casual purchasers of cosmetics to establish that they are buying a product that has been developed in a fashion that they find ethically acceptable. Similarly, it is difficult for employers to be sure that they are recruiting junior employees who are sufficiently talented and industrious. In such situations, economic agents seek out counterparties whose behaviour they regard as predictable. The cosmetics buyer might elect to buy from the Body Shop, and the employer might choose a graduate from a tough degree course at a highly selective university. This is the sense in which we use the word 'reputation'. For us, reputation tells economic actors what to expect of counterparties to transactions that have hard-to-quantify or hard-to-measure qualities.

This definition has some immediate corollaries. First, it is meaningless to talk of 'reputation' in situations where measurement is easy and contracting is straightforward. The UK does not have a reputation for inclement weather because it is easy to measure its weather; the UK has inclement weather. Equally, it is meaningless to speak of reputation in situations that are ruled entirely by chance: a person might have been a lucky gambler, but if they are ascribed a reputation for good luck, they are granted a supernatural ability to influence the behaviour of the dice. Second, a reputation accrues to a particular attribute or quality. The Body Shop has a reputation for a particular response to ethical challenges; this reputation is distinct from any reputation that it might have for helpful staff, or for soaps that smell nice. Any of these reputations could be strengthened or impaired independently of the others. Third, reputations are hard to acquire. An individual can state that he intends to behave in a particular way, or a firm can adopt a particular policy, but, precisely because reputation concerns behaviour that is hard to assess, it will take a long time for either to acquire a reputation for this type of behaviour. Because reputations are rare, they can command a substantial price premium in markets where confidence in counterparties is particularly important. The flip side of this observation is that reputations are easy to break. A single unfavourable experience of a reputable firm might be enough to break its counterparties' confidence in its actions, and hence to destroy its reputation. For an example of this effect, we need look no further than the demise of the accounting firm Arthur Andersen.

The role of reputation in finance is clear. Financial transactions are characterised by massive asymmetries of information and of understanding. It is almost impossible for a corporation's officers to be sure that its first public offering is properly marketed or valued; investors seldom understand the securities that they buy as well as the firm issuing them or the bank selling them; corporate treasurers may struggle to make sense of the myriad risk-management solutions available to them, and later to determine whether the chosen solution was effective; most of the parties involved in a takeover bid have incomplete information. In each of these situations, the parties to a transaction rely upon third parties to work hard on their behalf, and to give them accurate and unbiased advice; in most situations, it will be impossible after the fact to check that either requirement was fulfilled. Financial intermediaries therefore rely upon their reputations to reassure clients of appropriate behaviour. As in other fields, financial reputations are hard to acquire. And, given the scale and importance of many financial transactions, financial reputations generate high quasi-rents.

How did we get here?

Although many of the big names in investment banking have not changed in more than half a century, the firms that bear them have changed dramatically. One of the few threads connecting the small, relatively poorly capitalised partnerships of the past to the huge, highly capitalised, multinational behemoths that they have become is the reputation that attaches to their names. In a recent book, two of us trace the evolution of investment banking reputations from the end of the 18th century.[7]

Investment banking has its origins not in financial trade, but in the transatlantic cotton and dry goods trade of the 19th century.[8] The merchants involved in this trade operated in the face of rudimentary communications systems (messages initially travelled in sailing boats) and ineffective systems of international and commercial law.[9] They responded to these strictures by creating networks of counterparties upon whom they could rely without recourse to the courts, and by being such a counterparty themselves.[10] Reliability was the basis of continued participation in these networks, and hence of doing business. Long before their primary business was financial, firms like NM Rothschild & Sons, Baring Brothers & Co and Brown, Shipley & Co were concerned primarily with reputation maintenance.

The move away from trading goods to trading exclusively in financial securities was a response to innovations in technology and in law.[11] The first transatlantic cable became operational in 1866, and the competitive advantage that the transatlantic traders could derive from their ability to sustain reputational trade in information was massively reduced. At the same time, the law of contract and the courts that enforced it became sufficiently advanced for cross-border merchants to rely upon it in commercial relationships.[12] It became easier to enter the Atlantic trading market, and the returns to be derived from a reputation in that market were correspondingly reduced. It was natural for the early traders to concentrate upon finance, where there were massive informational asymmetries and non-existent bankruptcy laws, and where, as a result, the returns to a good reputation were correspondingly high. And the pursuit of reputational quasi-rents remained a defining feature of investment banking for the following century.

Many of the features of early investment banks can be understood in terms of the importance of reputation in generating superior returns. For example, investment banks in the US and the UK were all organised as partnerships or closely held private companies until the 1970s. Partnership firms are run by their owners, who can hope to sell their stakes to a new generation of partners only if their reputational assets remain intact. They therefore have strong incentives to maintain their reputation over the long term, even at the expense of shorter-term gain.[13] In short, the partnership evolved in banking and other professional services firms as a mechanism to protect reputations.

Reputation in financial markets

Figure 8.1 Advances in processing power, 1950–2001, MSOPS

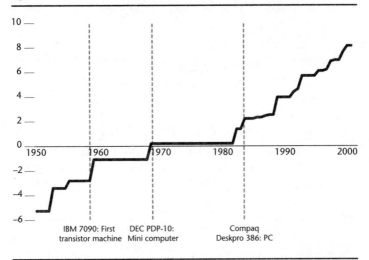

The shift away from the partnership form began with the 1971 flotation of Merrill Lynch, and continued for the following two decades. If the partnership form was such an effective mechanism for preserving institutional reputation, why did the banks choose to abandon it in favour of the joint-stock corporate form? The answer is that, precisely as they did in the middle of the 19th century, investment banks were facing massive technological shifts. These occurred in two fields: computing and financial engineering.

Information technology powered a modern industrial revolution in the second half of the 20th century. Figure 8.1 illustrates a time series of the most powerful computers available in the second half of the 20th century as measured by a standardised measurement, millions of instructions per second (MSOP). Figure 8.2 illustrates changes to the cost of computing over the same period.[14] The massive advances in computer power, starting about a decade before flotation began, were

Figure 8.2 **Cost of computing, 1950–2001, cost per million instructions**

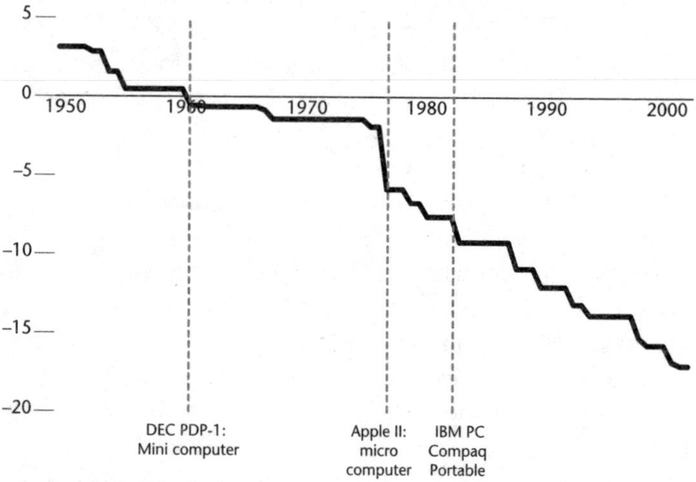

punctuated by such advances as the 1959 introduction of transistor technology into computing and the large-scale availability of desktop processing in the 1980s.

Computerisation was initially of particular importance to retail-oriented firms like Merrill Lynch, which performed high volumes of small-scale trades. These firms could use computers to realise significant economies of scale in their back offices. But computers were initially expensive, and they could realise these economies only by issuing new share capital and jettisoning the partnership form.

Computerisation was less obviously relevant to wholesale investment banks like Morgan Stanley. These firms were engaged in relationship-based business in which economies of scale were harder to achieve. These economies of scale became possible, and computers became important, in such firms as a result of advances in financial economics in the 1970s. The discovery in the early 1970s of option pricing formulae[15] was the first of a series of advances in quantitative finance that rendered precise and susceptible to measurement and contract several activities that previously had been tacit and relationship-based. These tasks were now susceptible to computerisation, and the increasing availability of cheap computers enabled players in these fields to realise economies of scale that had not existed a decade before.

These changes are of particular relevance in the light of the earlier discussion of reputation. By making measurement and contract easier in finance, financial engineering and computerisation rendered it easier for counterparties to form reasonable expectations of one another's behaviour. As a consequence, reputation became a less valuable commodity in these markets. At the same time, the massive scale that commoditised financial markets demanded was impossible to achieve in a partnership. It was inevitable that wholesale investment banking firms would abandon the partnership form.[16]

The trends that we have identified in investment banking were also at work in the commercial banking sector. Commercial banks are historically concerned with the production of information, which they use to screen and monitor their borrowers.[17] Advances in information technology therefore had a profound effect on commercial banks. They generated economies of scale, for example through the use of ATMs and offshore call centres, and they enabled the adoption of credit-scoring technologies to assess loan requests from individuals and small companies. To some extent, these technologies have substituted computerised decision-making for the judgement of the relationship-focused commercial banker. Large banks can use their computer systems to apportion capital among many loan officers. This has a cost, in that the loan officer's soft information is less likely to feature in the decision-making,[18] but it is one that commercial banks seem willing to take in pursuit of the economies of scale that

Figure 8.3 **Changing relationship strength in investment banking**

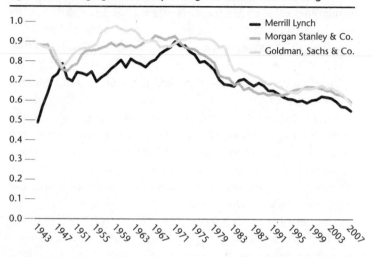

computers bring. Increased computerisation has also coincided with a greater availability of credit.

A bank's relationship strength with a counterparty is defined to be the dollar fraction of the counterparty's public offerings for which the bank is bookrunner. Figure 8.3 shows average relationship strengths for each bank.

In short, the reduced emphasis upon reputation in financial markets is not a recent phenomenon. It has its genesis in technological changes that date back at least 50 years. Further evidence of this trend appears in Figure 8.3, which shows relationship strength from 1940 to 2008 for three major investment banks.[19] In the early part of the chart, all the banks have a high relationship strength measure: this is consistent with the retention of clients in long-lived, close relationships that rely upon reputation. Relationship strength starts to drop in the 1970s; by the beginning of the 21st century, relationship strengths were much lower, as bank clients became less reliant upon the close relationships that foster reputations, and instead began to shop around for their underwriters.

Conflict in modern banks

The technological changes discussed above opened the door for commercial bank entry into investment banking. Historically, commercial banks' reputations were not obviously fungible with those of investment banks. But they had large balance sheets, and they had a great deal of data about the performance of their borrowers. In some fields, most notably bond underwriting, computerisation allowed them to substitute the latter qualities for a long-lived market reputation. As a result, competition in these fields has intensified. Furthermore, the economies of scale and scope that come with computerisation have generated a technological impetus towards bank consolidation, and the creation of large and complex financial institutions that provide everything from traditional lending and mergers and acquisitions (M&A) advisory work to complex derivatives structuring. The average size of the largest three banks in the US increased by a factor of 2.3 between 1988 and 1997, and by a factor of 2.3 between 1997 and 2007; all the ten largest banks had assets of over $100 billion in 2007, while only Citigroup exceeded this figure in 1988.[20] Of the largest US banks, only Citigroup has more assets than any of the largest European banks.[21] Some of this expansion reflects economies of scale, although it is partially a consequence of the distortional effects of mispriced deposit-insurance protection.[22]

Large and complex financial firms present governance challenges that go beyond the simple fact of their scale. These challenges were thrown into sharp relief by the civil complaint that the American Securities and Exchange Commission (SEC) filed against Goldman Sachs in April 2010. The claim alleged a fraud by Goldman in connection with a 2007 securitisation.[23]

The ABACUS transaction, while highly complex, was not particularly innovative, and its execution was not unusual. The trade allowed a hedge fund manager, John Paulson, to take a short position on a portfolio of Baa2-rated residential mortgage-backed securities (RMBSs). A German Bank, IKB Deutsche Industriebank, and ACA Management took the other side of the trade, and Goldman intermediated the deal. The SEC claimed that Goldman misled investors by claiming that ACA selected the RBMSs at the heart of the deal, while failing to disclose that Paulson played a significant role in the selection of the securities. Goldman was also accused of misrepresenting Paulson's position by giving the impression that he had a long, and not a short, position. Goldman ultimately agreed a $550 million settlement with the SEC.

The public reaction to this deal was critical. During the Senate Homeland Security and Governmental Affairs Subcommittee on Permanent Investigations on Wall Street and the Financial Crisis: The Role of Investment Banks, Senator Claire McCaskill characterised securitisations as 'instruments that are created so that people can bet on them', and continued 'you had less oversight than a pit boss in Las Vegas'. John Ensign, senator for Nevada, responded with the observation that 'most people in Las Vegas would take offence at having Wall Street compared to Las Vegas'.[24]

We have seen no suggestion that Goldman did a poor job of structuring or transacting the ABACUS transaction. Yet politicians and the public appear to believe that Goldman had some additional, fiduciary, duty, which it violated. If its counterparties believed this then, by acting contrary to their expectations, Goldman would have undermined its reputation.

Lloyd Blankfein, chairman and chief executive of Goldman Sachs, did not appear to share these concerns in his testimony to the US Senate Homeland Security and Governmental Affairs Subcommittee cited above. He argued: 'What the clients are buying ... is an exposure. The thing we are selling to them is supposed to give them the risk they want. They are not coming to us to represent what our views are ... They shouldn't care.'

Blankfein appears to draw no distinction between a standard share transaction, for which it would be illegal for Goldman to disclose the details of its counterparties, and the complex ABACUS deal, where the SEC appeared to believe that such a disclosure was Goldman's duty. This is a critical point. If the counterparties to the ABACUS deal did not expect Goldman to fulfil any role beyond structuring and executing the deal, then, quite apart from any legal questions, a failure to provide detailed information about the other parties to the deal did not violate expectations, and hence could not impair Goldman's reputation. The rather limited evidence available suggests that this interpretation of the facts is the right one: the more informed commentators are about the securitisation market, the less likely they appear to be to believe that Goldman acted inappropriately.[25]

The ABACUS transaction highlights a fundamental conflict in today's universal banks. On the one hand, these banks continue to work in a purely advisory capacity in arenas like the M&A and IPO (initial public offering) market where the quality of their advice is both critically important and hard to measure. Banks in these markets rely heavily on a reputation for fair dealing and careful attention to the fiduciary elements of their relationships. On the other hand, the same banks are active in purely arm's-length securities markets, where the most important determinants of success are speed of execution and accurate pricing. Precisely because these requirements are more easily measured, and hence are more susceptible to formal contract, the reputational needs of these businesses are very different. Somewhere between these two extremes lies a grey area, where the precise expectations of customers are less obvious, and where reputation is harder to manage. We would argue that highly complex, and theoretically codifiable, deals like ABACUS lie in this grey area. While a client could theoretically figure out the details of such a deal for itself, it might still expect guidance from its bank. The conflict between Goldman Sachs and the SEC hinged upon whether such expectations were reasonable.

In short, big bank activities can be divided into transactional businesses, where scale and technical competence are the main factors that create success, and reputational businesses, where long-term relationships and the satisfaction of hard-to-quantify expectations are the crucial factors. As the trends identified in the previous section continue to play out, more and more businesses will fall into the former category. Blankfein's 2006 appointment to the CEO role at Goldman is evidence of this trend: after his arrival, Goldman was controlled for the first time entirely by traders. This is not a coincidence. It reflects economic imperatives.

Notwithstanding the apparent drift towards transactional business, managing the reputational conflict within their businesses remains a central challenge for large banks. A strict separation of activities is almost impossible to achieve and, in any case, a large bank's brand has a wide reach, so that actions in one part of the bank affect the operations of other parts. The post-1990 rise of boutique, advisory-only, investment banks reflects one response to this problem: if a boutique does no principal business, it faces none of the conflicts that confront a big bank. But, at the same time, the boutique lacks the market intelligence and execution abilities that a large bank has. And the bank's decision-making is further complicated by rapid changes to the regulatory landscape.

Regulation and reputation

The technological advances outlined earlier that drove the phenomena discussed in the previous section have also affected the regulatory landscape:

- First, like bankers, regulators have been able to harness advances in computation and financial engineering. For example, capital regulations are now predicated upon value at risk (VaR) data generated by bank risk-management systems. VaR-type approaches have been adopted to quantify and regulate phenomena like fraud and operational controls that are not obviously their original target.
- Second, regulators are starting to deal with the reputational conflicts that attracted the SEC's attention in the ABACUS transaction.

The first of these phenomena is important, although it lies outside the scope of this chapter. For example, if they use bank systems for regulation, will supervisors correctly account for the externalities that are the appropriate focus of their attention, but are by definition of no interest to the banks they regulate?[26] Similarly, does the use of privately generated data in regulation have a deleterious effect on the incentives of those who generate and use that information?[27] It is fair to ask whether, in focusing upon data that are easily quantified, supervisors have underemphasised soft information. Lastly, we are surely not the only people who suspect that, at times, regulators have been seduced by elegant mathematics into viewing the financial markets in terms of the precise physical sciences, rather than as messy, complex, social phenomena that are driven by the expectations and beliefs of multiple unpredictable individuals.[28]

The second phenomenon is directly related to the argument in this chapter. When parties rely on reputationally intermediated contracts, they do so in the shadow of the formal law. A formal law is unlikely to reflect all the subtleties of a reputational transaction. It may prevent deals from happening in situations where they are desirable, for example by shielding counterparties from the reputational consequences of reneging on an agreement: this happens, for example, when a crude regulation confers a de facto monopoly upon a market player, such as a credit-rating agency. In short, the socially superior outcomes attainable via reputational contracts can be crowded out by crude formal laws.[29]

But if formal laws can undermine reputational contracting, they can also facilitate trade by making it easier for counterparties to write black-letter contracts and enforce them. Naturally, this is most clearly the case in situations where such contracts are viable and economically useful: in other words, when information is measurable and can be codified, and when the courts are able to interpret it.

Regulators therefore face a trade-off. They can take advantage of recent advances in information technology and financial engineering to create an institutional framework within which banks and their clients can use formal, black-letter contracts to fix expectations, and hence to underpin welfare-enhancing trade. We should not underestimate the benefits to be gained from this type of framework. Nevertheless, such regulations have the potential to replace effective and nuanced arrangements that rely on reputation and tacit agreement with cruder, black-letter contracts. The immediate cost of this type of crowding-out is the failure to achieve valuable cooperation, with a consequential short-term loss of reputation. A less obvious long-term consequence is that unused reputations atrophy. Reputations are hard to build, so this consequence would be hard to reverse. The long-term cost of excessive codification in financial regulation is therefore the destruction of private reputations in financial markets.

Conclusion

Reputations are valuable in situations of incomplete information and weak contracting because they tell the parties to a social interaction what to expect. They are therefore of particular relevance in financial markets, which have always been riven by information asymmetries and conflicts of interest.

Reputation remains important in financial markets, but its role has been steadily changing for several decades. Advances in computer technology and financial engineering have enabled codification of many things that previously could not be measured. Businesses that were once the preserve of the relationship banker are now executed on an arm's-length basis in the dealing room. Traditional notions of reputation are less valuable in this type of business than financial scale, technical virtuosity and rapid execution. As a result, banks have adopted new organisational forms that downplay reputation. The partnership died in investment banking because it was no longer as useful to bankers.

Large-scale computerisation has broken down the reputational barriers to entry in many businesses, and it has created economies of scale and scope. In the past two decades there has been a massive increase in the size of, and the range of activities performed by, banks. And the new universal banks face a conflict between the reputational needs of their advisory businesses and those of their codified trading businesses. There is a danger that the needs of the advisory business will be subsumed by those of the trading activities.

None of this is to suggest that, left to themselves, bankers will necessarily resolve the above trade-off incorrectly. If computerisation and financial engineering have advanced to such a pitch of perfection that they can substitute for traditional tacit reputational arrangements, then it is right that they do so, and that we realise the economies of scale that computers generate. If reputations retain an economic value in some businesses, then, as in the case of the boutique investment banks, those businesses can break away from the universal banks. The flip side of this observation is that there is no a priori reason to believe that regulators can necessarily resolve these conflicts more effectively than the bankers who are closest to the problem. The Vickers Report argues for greater separation between commercial and investment banking.[30] This recommendation reflects the danger that a safety net intended for depositors might be extended to securities traders. But the benefits that could be derived from preventing this abuse should be weighed against the potential costs of restricting the scope of the contract by administrative fiat.

We are witnessing Schumpeterian creative destruction.[31] It is too early to say how it will play out. Particularly as we design new financial regulations, we should appreciate our epistemic limitations. It is tempting to attempt to substitute for an apparent reduction in reputational concerns with detailed and codified regulation. In the newer, more transactional, trading-room businesses, this is a reasonable approach. But legislators face a difficult balancing act: detailed legislation that encroaches upon tacit and reputational businesses may serve to undermine, and ultimately extinguish, the reputational concerns that make those businesses successful.

9

Nostra culpa

HUGO DIXON

The banking industry has come in for a lot of flak since the credit crisis started four years ago. It will come in for more over the next few years. Weak economies in industrialised countries and the raging crisis in the euro zone virtually guarantee that. The media, politicians and the general public will not be able to resist making bankers the whipping boys.

Investment bankers are not, of course, the only culprits. But they do bear some of the blame for the current mess because they ran excessive risks in the bubble years. They are easy to kick because they earn so much at a time when others are suffering from austerity and high unemployment. What really sticks in the craw is that banks have continued to pay their employees well despite requiring bail-outs. This argument is unlikely to go away, at least in Europe, as yet more cash infusions from the European Central Bank and capital injections from governments will be required to prevent lenders from collapsing.

The anti-banker backlash has three main parts: regulation, taxes and rhetoric. The most that the industry can hope for is to take the edge off these attacks.

Tougher regulation is required to prevent banks running amok in the future and so requiring bail-outs. There is nothing the industry can do to prevent the broad thrust of this — tougher capital and liquidity rules, living wills and more intrusive supervision. The industry's best argument is that the regulation should not be so harsh that it prevents banks from serving the real economy.

There are two main motivations for higher taxes: governments are desperate for money and banks are unpopular. So we have had windfall payroll taxes in the UK and various levies around Europe. The industry's best hope is to prevent a Tobin Tax, given that both the United States and the UK are opposed.

As for rhetoric, well, bankers are just going to have to live with being the butt of jokes.

But if they are even to mitigate this backlash, banks need to find a more sensitive way of speaking to the public. This is why I have penned the following letter from the chairman of an imaginary bank to the leaders of the G20.

***

To: Barack Obama and other G20 leaders
From: Humboldt Pye, chairman, First Reform Bank, and other leading bank chairmen
Dear Mr President,

I'm writing an open letter to you and other G20 leaders on behalf of the chairmen of the world's leading banks to say sorry.

We do not think banks are to blame for every ill the world currently faces, as the Occupy Wall Street Protests and their kin in other countries suggest. A balanced audit would attribute responsibility to policymakers too: you set the rules of the game that we so craftily exploited; you borrowed too much to avoid levying taxes; and your central banks inflated the bubble with low interest rates. Even the public had a hand in the current mess: excess spending in some countries and inadequate taxpaying in others allowed people to consume more than they were producing.

But we accept we are not in a position to lecture the rest of society. Our own share of the blame is big.

We do, though, feel that a healthy banking industry is an essential part of a healthy economy. Bad practices must be rooted out. But it is not in anybody's interests that the banking industry is hobbled or that the backlash against finance is so severe that it sweeps away what is good in capitalism. We are, therefore, determined to make amends — starting with a full and frank apology — in the hope that this will create a climate in which we can all work together to pull through these difficult times.

Bubble trouble

During the bubble years, we paid little attention to the public interest. We focused first on our own pay packages and then on profits for our shareholders. In so far as we thought about the wider interest, we comforted ourselves with the belief that financial markets were efficient and free markets were the best way of generating wealth. So, if we were pursuing our self-interest, the world must by definition be getting better.

This ideology of greed was convenient. It meant we didn't bother to think about whether our fancy new products would blow up. We didn't have any qualms about lobbying governments to deregulate financial services. And we poached some of the smartest regulators by paying them many times their public-sector salaries and so were able to run rings around those who were left.

We didn't care much about the future: after all, market prices discounted that perfectly. We didn't care that much about the past either, except in so far as our rocket scientists crunched through historical data to plug into their ever-so-clever models.

There were multiple flaws in this intellectual edifice. But contrary to popular belief, the weakness was not so much the failure of the market as the failure to apply the market. There were three main distortions.

First, central banks, especially the US Federal Reserve, were always cutting interest rates at the first sign of trouble. We loved that. But it meant we were lulled into taking excess risk by the belief that nanny was always there to rescue the markets.

A second, equally damaging distortion was the notion that governments would bail out any banks that were in danger of failing. Again, this blunted fear throughout our industry as well as among our bondholders and shareholders. We were able to raise funds on cheap terms, leverage ourselves to the gills and finance long-term lending with short-term borrowing — all without the market batting an eyelid.

Lastly, our compensation practices amounted to 'heads I win, tails you lose' bets. If our gambles paid off, we went laughing all the way to the bank. If they didn't, the tab was left with shareholders and ultimately taxpayers. We spun the roulette wheel.

Après le déluge

Our apology, though, can't stop here. In some ways, how we behaved after the bubble burst was even worse. We have been ungrateful for all the help we've received. Without government and central-bank assistance, most of us would have gone bankrupt. The support was extraordinary: massive infusions of cheap liquidity from monetary authorities; capital injections from governments, often on extremely generous terms; no haircuts for bondholders when banks got into trouble; and state guarantees to help us raise new debt.

Of course, Lehman Brothers was allowed to go bust in such an uncontrolled fashion that the rest of us were left reeling — and that was a big government error. But we didn't do much to organise our own lifeboat either. What's more, we benefited hugely from bail-outs of other teetering giants, notably AIG — a rescue that saved some of us billions of dollars.

Despite all this aid, we have kept paying our staff mega packages. This is partly because we denied the full extent of the help we were receiving and continue to receive. Whenever markets temporarily rebounded (often as a result of your central banks' liquidity injections) we patted ourselves on the back for being so clever and rewarded ourselves handsomely.

We justified these actions on the basis that we had to pay the market rate for the job. If we didn't reward talented bankers, they would run off to rival institutions. And we couldn't club together to keep compensation down, could we? That would be a buyers' cartel. There was some truth in these arguments, but it is also the case that we were hopelessly conflicted. We didn't want to see compensation drop.

This greed has enraged people and helped provoke the current backlash. Countries have imposed special taxes on the industry and pretty much everywhere the regulatory noose has been tightening. We are not so naive as to think we can swim against this tide, but we have sought to delay and dilute the most significant changes to capital and liquidity rules. The reason is simple. Leverage boosts returns and short-term funds are cheaper than long-term money. The more we have to jack up capital ratios and boost liquidity reserves, the less profitable we'll be.

We have tried especially hard to wriggle out of anything that smacks of nationalisation. Those of us that haven't avoided this fate have had tough controls imposed on bonuses and dividends. The rest of us have therefore preferred to do anything to escape the state's embrace. This includes shrinking our balance sheets rapidly. That allows us to boost capital 'ratios' without issuing extra equity. Given the binge of the bubble years, deleveraging is appropriate. But rushing the process is probably tightening credit conditions and worsening the economic difficulties.

During this whole process, we've communicated terribly. Not that even a great orator like you, Mr President, would have found this easy. The public assumes that everything we say is self-serving. But a leadership vacuum compounded this problem. Most of us were too cowardly to speak up. The few who did got pilloried — like Goldman Sachs' Lloyd Blankfein when he made a bad-taste joke about how he was doing 'God's work'.

That pretty much left J.P. Morgan's Jamie Dimon to fill the void. For a while, he did a valiant job of speaking up for the industry in a down-to-earth manner. But too many flattering profiles about how he was a latter-day John Pierpont Morgan saving the financial system may have gone to his head. His verbal assault on the Bank of Canada governor, Mark Carney, at the International Monetary Fund meeting in September shocked even other bankers.

Pressing reset

We would now like to press the reset button and develop a new, healthier relationship between the banking industry and society.

At the heart of this will be the regulatory regime you are developing — in particular, measures to make sure that no bank in future is too big to fail. Capital buffers must be increased and reliance on short-term money decreased so banks are less likely to fail; banks need to develop credible resolution plans so they can be safely packed off to the knacker's yard without dragging down the rest of the financial system if they do run into trouble; and bondholders need to be bailed in when banks go bust so that taxpayers don't have to bail us out.

You are already onto all this. Our pledge is that we will cooperate as you institute these changes rather than fight them every step of the way.

We will also try harder to explain what we do with the aim of showing how we add value to society. This will involve a sea change in our culture. We will have to be much more transparent and think more deeply about what we do.

Our core functions are essential. We enable people and companies to make payments for goods and services; we help people save; we play an important role in allocating capital to companies that need to invest; our products can help businesses and investors cut risk.

But we accept that some of our complex products had perverse results. We didn't even properly understand them ourselves. If we can't in future explain to an intelligent layman how what we do helps society, we should stop doing it.

We do not, of course, expect the public to believe our protestations of better behaviour. So our senior executives are forgoing bonuses for at least two years. We are also going to squeeze cash compensation for other staff. Overall, the banking industry will shrink. We hope the public will in time appreciate that this leopard can change its spots.

Yours sincerely
Humboldt Pye

Notes

1 Banking in a market economy – the international agenda

1 See *The Bank of England, Prudential Regulation Authority: Our approach to banking supervision*, May 2011.
2 See Goodhart, C.A.E., *The Basel Committee on Banking Supervision: A history of the early years 1974–1997*, August 2011.
3 See Tucker, P.M.W., *Macroprudential policy: building financial stability institutions*, April 2011.
4 *Report of the Hong Kong Securities Review Committee*, 1988, paragraph 3.21. I worked for the SRC.
5 See Tucker, P.M.W., *Clearing houses as system risk managers*, June 2011.
6 See *Shadow Banking: Strengthening Oversight and Regulation Recommendations of the Financial Stability Board*, October 2011.
7 Blunden G., 'Supervision and Central Banking', *Bank of England Quarterly Bulletin*, August 1987.
8 See Tucker, P.M.W., *Mitigating Systemic Risk: A Role for Securities Regulators*, February 2011.
9 See Gennaioli, N., Shleifer, A. and Vishny, R., *Neglected Risks, Financial Innovation, and Financial Fragility*, September 2010. See also Tucker, P.M.W., *Reforming Finance*, February 2011.

3 Risk in financial institutions – is it managed?

1 See the famous statement by Lord Turner, chairman of the Financial Services Authority, calling some of the City's activities 'socially useless'.
2 See numerous documents from the Basel Committee; also from the Senior Supervisors Group, *Risk Management Lessons from the Global Banking Crisis of 2008*, 21 October 2009. On the broader issue of internal governance, see European Banking Authority, *Guidelines on Internal Governance*, 27 September 2011.

3 See IIF, *Principles of Conduct and Recommendations in Final Report of the Committee on Market Best Practices*, July 2008, updated December 2009 in *Reform of the Financial Services Industry: Strengthening Practices for a More Stable System*, December 2009.

4 For methods of identifying these links see Financial Stability Board, *Understanding Financial Linkages: A Common Data Template for Global Systemically Important Banks*, 6 October 2011.

5 Proposal for a directive, 'CRD IV', 20 July 2011 Com (2011) 453 final, 2011/0203 (COD), especially Article 75. 'Ensure effective and prudent management of an institution' and further 'the management body shall have the overall responsibility for the institution, including approving and overseeing the implementation of the institution's strategic objectives, risk strategy and internal governance'. These rules are addressed to the 'management body', which would include the board in the unitary systems and the management committee in the two-tier systems (see § 5.3 of the explanatory memorandum to CRD IV; compare European Banking Authority, *Guidelines on Internal Governance*, nt. 2, § 10).

6 See Hartmann, Wolfgang, *Aufgaben und Rolle des Risikoausschusses von Banken*, in Hopt, K.J. and Wohlmannstetter, G. (eds), *Handbuch Corporate Governance von Banken*, Vahlen Beck, 2011, pp. 528–82.

7 See Schmittmann, Stefan, *Die Rolle des Chief Risk Officer under Corporate Governance Gesichtspunkten*, in Hopt and Wohlmannstetter (eds), op. cit., pp. 528–82 481–92.

8 This aspect is highlighted in Institute of International Finance, *Implementing Robust Risk Appetite Frameworks to Strengthen Financial Institutions*, June 2011.

9 This point has not been stated in this way in the CRD4 proposal, but may be good practice. CRD4 defines the function as 'identifying, measuring, and reporting on risk exposures'. But it states that the CRO should be involved 'in all material risk management decisions', which might mean that he would not be involved in the business decisions themselves. Compare in the similar sense: European Banking Authority, *Guidelines on Internal Governance*, nt. 2, § 27.4.

10 'which shall have sufficient authority, stature, resources and access to the management' and 'independent senior executive with distinct responsibility for the risk management function body', according to Article 75(5) of the proposed CRD4.

11 This is the case in 92% of the top 25 European banks, according to an investigation by Nestor Advisors, *Bank Boards After the Flood*, October 2010, p. 12. In a worldwide survey, 'Making strides in financial services risk management', covering 60 large banks, the IIF and Ernst & Young found 86% had constituted a separate risk committee. Strikingly, the board approves the CRO's remuneration in 72% of these cases. But the CRO should also be at the appropriate level of seniority in the organisation.

Notes

12 No removal 'without prior approval of the management body', states Article 75(5) of the directive. The risk committee would normally play an important role, but the CRO's appointment is not necessarily a board matter, at least according to the directive.

13 Article 88(2)(a) CRD IV.

14 See SSG, *Observations on Developments in Risk Appetite Frameworks and IT Infrastructure*, 23 December 2010, p. 9, citing career advancement as an incentive, but also dismissal for those who disregard the framework.

15 CGFS, 'Macroprudential instruments and frameworks: a stocktaking of issues and experiences', Paper 38, May 2010; and IIF, *Macroprudential Oversight, An Industry Perspective*, Submission to the International Authorities, July 2011, especially pp. 9 and 22.

16 For the relative importance of these different factors see observations by KPMG Australia, *Understanding and Articulating Risk Appetite*, 2008.

17 Some of these and their methodologies have been dealt with in the CRD, implementing the Basel II Accord.

18 CRD IV, Article 77.

19 'In particular, internal methodologies shall not rely solely or mechanistically on external ratings. Where own funds requirements are based on a rating by an External Credit Assessment Institution (ECAI) or based on the fact that an exposure is unrated, institutions shall use their own methodologies in order to assess the appropriateness of the rank-ordering of credit risk implicit in those own funds requirements and take the result into account in their allocation of internal capital.' Article 77(b).

20 Article 78.

21 Article 79.

22 Article 80.

23 Article 82.

24 Article 83.

25 Article 85.

26 Striking examples of legal risks with a systemic dimension are found in the Netherlands, the so-called Legio Lease affair (equity leasing contracts), see nl.wikipedia.org/wiki/Aandelenlease-affaire), or in the case of the *woekerpolissen* (usurious policies), see nl.wikipedia.org/wiki/Woekerpolisaffaire — the latter potentially gravely damaging a large part of the insurance sector. More recently, the use of interest rate swaps with local communities ('Province of Pisa', Consiglio di Stato, Section V, nr 5032 of 7 July 2011), or with unsophisticated investors ('Ille Papier', Bundesgerichtshof Decision of 22 March 2011 — XI ZR 33/1), which in both cases were held invalid but led to fear of massive damages.

27 For the effects of private benefits on the pricing of the shares, see Gilson, R., *Controlling Shareholders and Corporate Governance: Complicating the Comparative Taxonomy*, August 2005, ECGI, Law Working Paper No. 49/2005.

28 See International Auditing Standard (ISA) 315.5.

29 Article 77(3).
30 Article 46 of the 4th Directive on Company Law.
31 Article 46 (a) (1) C of the 4th Directive on Company Law.
32 CEBS (now EBA), *Guidelines for Implementation of the Framework for Consolidated Financial Reporting* (FinRep), March 2009.
33 SSG, nt. 14, p. 14; see also IIF and McKinsey, *Risk IT and Operations: Strengthening Capabilities*, 21 June 2011.
34 Ernst & Young and IIF, Making Strides In Financial Services Management, 2011.

6 Megatrends shaping the corporate banking landscape – a European outlook

1 See *After the Storm: Creating Value in Banking 2010*, BCG report, February 2010.

8 Reputation in financial markets

1 See L. Endlich, *Goldman Sachs: The Culture of Success*, Touchstone Press, 2000; and http://www2.goldmansachs.com/who-we-are/business-standards/business-principles/index.html
2 Alan Greenspan, 'Markets and the Judiciary', Sandra Day O'Connor Project Conference, 2 October 2008, www.law.georgetown.edu/news/documents/Greenspan.pdf
3 S.M. Davidoff, 'As Wall Street firms grow, their reputations are dying', *New York Times* DealBook, 26 April 2011, http://dealbook.nytimes.com/2011/04/26/as-wall-st-firms-grow-their-reputations-are-dying/
4 See C. Harper, 'Wall Street shareholders suffer losses partners never imagined', Bloomberg, 11 February 2011, http://www.bloomberg.com/apps/news/pid=20601109&sid=a8xWme0GUnco.
5 See S.M. Davidoff, 'A Partnership Solution for Investment Banks?', *New York Times* DealBook, 20 August 2008, http://dealbooknytimes.com/2008/08/20/a-partnership-solution-for-investment-banks/; M. Lewis, 'The End', Portfolio, 11 November 2008; L. Ribstein, 'Governance, the unincorporation and subprime', 23 August 2008, http://busmovie.typepad.com/ideoblog/2008/08/governance-the.html
6 These perspectives are surveyed in D. Lange, P.M. Lee., and Y. Dal, 'Organizational Reputation: A Review', *Journal of Management*, 37 (1), pp. 153–184.
7 A.D. Morrison and W.J. Wilhelm, Jr, *Investment Banking: Institutions, Politics, and Law*, OUP, 2007.
8 See Morrison and Wilhelm, op. cit., Chapter 4.
9 M.J. Horowitz, *The Transformation of American Law*, Harvard University Press, 1977.

Notes

10 Morrison and Wilhelm, op. cit., Chapter 5; and, in the 18th century, D. Hancock, *Citizens of the World: London Merchants and the Integration of the British Atlantic Community, 1735–1785*, CUP, 1995.

11 Morrison and Wilhelm, op. cit., pp. 157 – 160.

12 Horowitz, op. cit., p. 185; L.M. Friedman, *A History of American Law*, 3rd edn, Simon & Schuster, 2005, p. 204.

13 See A.D. Morrison and W.J. Wilhelm, Jr, 'Partnership Firms, Reputation, and Human Capital', *American Economic Review*, 94, 2004, pp. 1682 – 92.

14 The data are in W.D. Nordhaus, 'The progress of computing', Yale University working paper, 2001, Appendix 2. They exclude supercomputers, which were intended for large-scale scientific computation, and were not used in commercial applications for most of this period.

15 F. Black and M. Scholes, 'The pricing of options and corporate liabilities', *Journal of Political Economy*, 1973, 81, pp. 637 – 54; and R. Merton, 'On the pricing of corporate debt: The risk-structure of interest rates', *Journal of Finance*, 1974, 29, pp. 449 – 70.

16 For a detailed discussion of investment bank flotations, see A.D. Morrison and W.J. Wilhelm, Jr, 'The Demise of Investment Banking Partnerships: Theory and Evidence', *Journal of Finance*, 63, 2008, pp. 311 – 50.

17 See for example D.W. Diamond, 'Financial Intermediation and Delegated Monitoring', *Review of Economic Studies*, 51, 1984, pp. 393 – 414.

18 See A.N. Berger, N.H. Miller, M.A. Petersen, R.G. Rajan and J.C. Stein, 'Does function follow organizational form? Evidence from the lending practices of large and small banks', *Journal of Financial Economics*, 76, pp. 237 – 69.

19 For any client, the bank's relationship strength is the CPI-adjusted US dollar fraction of the client's deals for which the bank acts as bookrunner. For each bank, the graph shows the average relationship strength across all its clients. These data are taken from ongoing research work by Morrison and Wilhelm with Aaron Thegeya and Carola Schenone. The pattern exhibited for the banks illustrated in Figure 8.3 is replicated for every major bank.

20 R. DeYoung, 'Banking in the United States', in A.N. Berger, P. Molyneux and J.O.S. Wilson (eds), *The Oxford Handbook of Banking*, OUP, 2010.

21 J.P. Goddard, P. Molyneux and J.O.S. Wilson, 'Banking in the European Union', in *The Oxford Handbook of Banking*, op. cit.

22 For a discussion, see A.D. Morrison, 'Systemic Risks and the "Too-Big-To-Fail" Problem', *Oxford Review of Economic Policy*, 2011.

23 The discussion of this deal draws upon the analysis in S.M. Davidoff, A.D. Morrison and W.J. Wilhelm, Jr, 'Computerization and the ABACUS: Reputation, Trust, and Fiduciary Duties in Investment Banking', *Journal of Corporation Law*, 2011.

24 For further evidence of the public reaction to the Goldman case, see also F. Salmon, 'BP: Still not as evil as Goldman Sachs', Reuters, 11 June 2010,

http://blogs.reuters.com/felix-salmon/2010/06/11/bp-still-not-as-evil-as-goldman-sachs/

25 For survey evidence in support of this claim, see J.A. Grundfest, The United States Securities and Exchange Commission v. Goldman Sachs & Co. and Fabrice Toure, www.law.stanford.edu/../SEC%20Goldman%20 Complaint%20Analysis_Joe%20Grundfest.pdf

26 See Davidoff, Morrison and Wilhelm, op. cit.

27 See, for example, F. Partnoy, 'The Paradox of Credit Ratings', in R.M. Levich *et al.* (eds), *Ratings, Rating Agencies and the Global Financial System*, 2002.

28 For a more detailed discussion of this perspective, see A.D. Morrison, 'Ratings agencies, regulation, and financial market stability', in P. Booth (ed.), *Verdict on the Crash: Causes and Policy Implications*, Institute of Economic Affairs, 2009.

29 See, for example, Morrison and Wilhelm (2007), op. cit., pp. 57–8; Davidoff, Morrison and Wilhelm, op. cit.; L. Bernstein, 'Merchant Law in a merchant court: Rethinking the code's search for immanent business norms', *University of Pennsylvania Law Review*, 144, 1996, pp. 1765–821; and G. Baker, R. Gibbons, K.J. Murphy, 'Relational contracts and the theory of the firm', *Quarterly Journal of Economics*, 117, 2002, pp. 39 & 84.

30 Independent Commission on Banking, *Final Report*, September 2011.

31 J.A. Schumpeter, *Capitalism, Socialism, and Democracy*, Harper & Brothers, 1942, Chapter 7.

9 Nostra culpa

This is an edited version of an article that first appeared on Reuters' Breakingviews in October 2011.